For Elisabethann and Oisín
thank you for your love and support

# Rest in Peace

Marc Quaghebeur

# Rest in Peace

A Guide to Wills and Inheritance Tax in Belgium

taxation.be

Rest in Peace
Marc Quaghebeur

© by taxation.be, Brussels
Tel: +32.2.423.00.42
Fax: +32.2.706.47.54
info@taxation.be
www.taxation.be
Cover photo : © www.atomium.be - SABAM  Belgium 2013

ISBN 9789082047905
NUR 820
Wettelijk depot: D/2013/13.155/1

# CONTENTS

# INTRODUCTION

If you are a Belgian living in Belgium with no property or savings outside Belgium, not planning your estate need not have major consequences. The default rules are quite fair. When you pass away, everything goes to the family with some form of protection for your spouse or registered partner.

If you are living in Belgium because you are working here, you may have discovered that things are different from what you are used to in your home country. Things can also get a little bit more complex in other circumstances, for example, if you are about to inherit from your parents, if you have a holiday home in Italy and France, and bank accounts to pay for the charges.

That is before other complications can occur, such as a spouse with a different nationality, a parent living in France, children in Spain, Greece and Croatia, while you plan to retire in Italy.

In addition, the days when estate planning was just about limiting inheritance tax for a happy couple who have been married for forty years, with two well-adjusted children and four lovely grandchildren are long gone. Estate planning has become more complex. It is not only about planning around ever changing laws, but also around non-traditional families, estranged families, and everything in between.

The purpose of this book is to dissipate some misunderstandings and help you plan your estate.

## 10 COMMON MISUNDERSTANDINGS

1.    *"Surely, this does not concern me; I am not Belgian"*

Rules in Belgium do not apply only to Belgians. Inheritance rules and inheritance tax apply to everyone who lives in Belgium. Inheritance rules do not apply to real property in other countries – but other rules may apply there.

Even if you are not living here, you need to understand the Belgian rules if you have property in Belgium.

2.     *"I have no worries about inheritance tax. I have taken up domicile in Sweden and Sweden has no inheritance tax"*

It is correct that Sweden abolished inheritance tax in 2005, as did Austria, Cyprus, Estonia, Latvia, Malta, Portugal, Romania and the Slovak Republic.

However, if you have property in Belgium, it will pass to your heirs in accordance with Belgian law and Belgian inheritance tax will be due.

If you really are domiciled in Sweden, do you come back to Belgium every other week to be with your wife and children?

3.     *"I will just leave everything to my wife, and she will leave everything to me. When I am gone, she can then decide what she does with our money".*

That is not possible in Belgium. You have to leave a large percentage of your estate to your children; you cannot disinherit them. If you have three children, they must receive three quarters of your estate. Your spouse can only receive a quarter of your estate. Even then you have to make a will to give her that. If not, she only receives a *usufruct* on your estate.

4.     *"My wife and I made a will in Ireland to leave each other our house in Dublin. There is no inheritance tax between husband and wife there."*

That is correct. The Belgian rule that you cannot disinherit your children does not apply to property in Ireland; you and your wife can leave each other everything there. It is correct that, under Irish law, there is no inheritance tax between husband and wife.

Since you are resident in Belgium, your heirs will have to declare your entire estate in the inheritance tax return. Your estate does not include only your property in Belgium, but also your property in Dublin.

By way of relief against double taxation on inheritances, your heirs can deduct the Irish inheritance tax from the Belgian inheritance tax. However, if no inheritance tax is due in Ireland, you pay full inheritance tax in Belgium on that property.

5. *"My first wife took half of everything when we divorced in the U.K. Now I need to give some financial security to my new wife and our children. The children from my first marriage are well taken care of; they can just will inherit from their mother"*

Your child always remains your child. If you have two children from a first marriage and two from your second marriage, you have four children and they must inherit three quarters of your estate. You can only leave a quarter of your estate in full ownership to your second spouse. The children from your first marriage will inherit an equal share to that of the children of your second marriage in what the children inherit. That they have not kept in touch or that they will inherit from their mother does not change anything.

6. *"My husband and I divorced last year; it was not pleasant at all. Now I have a good job and I could finally buy a house. I want to leave my house to my daughter. She is three now; I do not want my husband to live in the house."*

If you and your husband have divorced, your husband will not inherit anything. However, if you die before your daughter is an adult her father will be her guardian. He can manage her assets and decide where she will live. He will take all decisions about her wellbeing and her possessions and he may even decide that it would be best for her if they lived in the house that you will leave to her. He even has the right to the income from your daughter's assets and the right to live in the house.

7. *"I work for the EU Commission. I joined from the U.K. so that my heirs will pay inheritance tax in the U.K. If I leave everything to my wife, we do not have to worry about Belgian inheritance tax.*

If you are an official of one of the EU Institutions, you keep your domicile in the country where you had it before you joined the Commission for income and inheritance tax purposes. Your heirs will not pay Belgian inheritance tax on your entire estate, only on the property you have in Belgium.

Keep in mind that the Belgian inheritance rules do apply. That means that your two children must receive at least two thirds of your estate. They cannot claim the exemption between husband and wife.

If your wife is working somewhere other than the EU Institutions, she does not keep her domicile in the U.K., she will be deemed to be domiciled in Belgium. That means she cannot claim the exemption either, because you do not have the same domicile anymore.

Do not forget that your estate is only exempted from Belgian inheritance tax because you do not have your domicile here. You only have that privilege as long as you work for the EU Institutions. If you stay in Belgium when you retire, you take up domicile in Belgium.

8. *"We have paid tax on my husband's company pension when he redeemed it upon retirement. That was last year; surely we do not have to pay inheritance tax as well"*

Unfortunately, sometimes both income tax and inheritance tax are due on the same pension.

If your husband had redeemed his company pension, he paid income tax. Belgian company pensions are geared to be redeemed at 65: the income tax rate is good (10%). However, that pension capital will be in his estate. It may still be sitting in his bank account or he may have invested it in Sicavs or in an insurance wrapper. It is for that reason that inheritance tax will be due.

When your husband received a monthly company pension, you will normally get a smaller company pension of your own, and you will have to declare that pension in your income tax return.

Normally, you do not need to declare that pension in his inheritance tax return. However, if your husband received his pension not as a retired employee but as a retired self-employed, you have to declare your own pension in the inheritance tax return and pay inheritance tax as well.

In addition, if your husband died before retirement age, his pension scheme may well pay a capital upon death. That capital will be liable to inheritance tax (if he was self-employed), but you will see that the pension plan will withhold income tax as well.

9.   *"My husband has set up his personal services company Jack O'Donnell SPRL and that works out very well. He saves on social security and tax. We have the house and the cars in the company and we pay little tax."*

Fortunately, he is still alive, and it is not too late to avoid making mistakes. He holds all the shares in his company and you do not have any for one of several reasons being because the firm he is working for does not allow you to hold any, because you work for the EU Institutions, or because he is not taking any risks and wants to keep control over his possessions, just in case the marriage breaks down.

If the shares are not community property, you do not own anything. What he holds is his and is passed on to his heirs in accordance with the Belgian inheritance rules. The shares are part of his estate and you may inherit the *usufruct* while the bare ownership goes to his children. In that case, who has the voting right in the company, check the articles of association, or have them adapted to take the right to vote away from the owners.

What happens if your husband is not there anymore to work and make the income that must pay off the mortgage on the house and the company cars? Hopefully he has thought of a company pension and that may pay you a capital to finance the loans. Do you want to keep the property in the company? If not, how do you want to take it out? If the children are under the age of 18, decision relating to their shares will require the authorisation of the justice of the peace.

If any of these scenarios sound familiar, then there may be something in this book for you.

Fortunately, if you know the problem, you can do something about it. You do not have to accept the standard answer. It is possible that you can find a solution that is not too difficult but that suits your purposes. That is what estate planning is all about in the first place. However, another common mistake is:

10.   *"If I read this book, I can do my own estate planning"*

This book is an introduction to estate planning in Belgium. I hope that it will get you started.

However, given the complex maze of laws (civil law, inheritance law, tax laws and inheritance tax, social security laws, etc…), it is recommended that you work with an experienced estate planning lawyer or notary.

Even then, if you have to take account of the laws of one or more countries, a small misstep or oversight can be very problematic and you may need a lawyer in another country to assist you.

This book will help you put the correct questions to your advisers.

# ESTATE PLANNING

Estate planning is in the first place about deciding who will get your estate, but it is much more. You may want to know what you are facing, or rather, what your heirs will be facing.

Estate planning is also about keeping assets in your estate by having appropriate insurance, by minimizing the inheritance tax on your estate, and planning for the management of your finances and your medical care in case you become incapacitated and cannot manage them for yourself.

If you have young children, estate planning is also planning for them if both their parents die before they become adults. You can use your will to help the justice of the peace court designate the adult who will raise the children and manage their assets. If you don't, the justice of the peace will decide who will play those critically important roles in your children's lives.

To a lesser degree, estate planning is also about preparing a living will, a document that spells out the kinds of life-sustaining medical care you do and do not want if you are terminally ill or injured and close to death.

In Belgium, you cannot make that many decisions, but a living will is much more important if you plan to retire in a country like the U.S. where that sort of medical care can be much more of a burden on your estate.

You will not relish the idea of estate planning. It is not only that it takes some work to get your affairs sorted out. It also means you have to acknowledge the fact that someday you will die, an unpleasant reality that we would all rather avoid.

However, given all of the very important things that estate planning can accomplish, preparing an estate plan is the responsible thing to do as a spouse, a partner, and as a parent.

## HOW DO I READ THIS BOOK?

Any book on estate planning must start with death and what happens thereafter. If you want to plan how you leave your estate to your loved ones, you need to know how your estate will be administered in Belgium, and to understand how your assets go to your heirs. In short, the red tape about Dealing with Death. Because you will not be there that is more a guideline to help your heirs, but it will help you to understand what they need to do.

If you plan to make a will, you need to understand Who inherits what if you do not make a will. If you want to change these rules, you can draw up a will. We will see how in Last Will And Testament. It is very important to understand what you can do and what you cannot do. "Forced Heirship", "Usufruct" and "Community Property" are notions that we will use regularly, we explain them in a separate chapter.

Inheritance tax is an important issue as well. Despite what you may have been told, the inheritance tax rates in Belgium are not the highest in Europe. It is true, the highest tax rate in Belgium is 80%, but that is only for bequests to strangers. Generally speaking, the average is much lower; in a standard family the average rate is between 10 and 20%. That compares quite favourably to the 40% inheritance tax rate in the U.K. (over the nil rate band of £325,000).

This book is written for people in one or other international situation. That is what Cross-Border Successions is about. Do the Belgian inheritance rules apply to assets I inherit in another country? Do they deal with my parents' inheritance? Is Belgian inheritance tax due on my property and my bank accounts outside Belgium? Officials of the EU Institutions are in a particular situation. They keep their domicile outside Belgium, and their heirs pay inheritance tax there. At the same time, they are liable to inheritance tax on the property they buy in Belgium.

If you do not wish to read this, you can skip to the chapter The Art of Estate Planning. This chapter gives a general introduction to estate planning techniques. Limiting inheritance tax is the most obvious purpose of any estate planning exercise, but there are many other reasons to plan your estate in advance.

We will then look at the various planning techniques. You can start by drawing up a will. If inheritance tax is an issue, you may well want to start planning ahead and donate your possessions before your death. For a married couple, a good piece of advice is to change your marriage contract. Finally, there are also different forms of contract that can be used, life insurance is an important one of them. Trusts and foundations are dealt with in more detail.

Finally, we give you some hints to help your heirs to understand what they need to do. Leaving this book in your files is a good starting point. We will suggest a form of personal affairs checklist and a personal affairs box.

You may also want to consider a living will. Anglo Saxon countries are well ahead of Belgium in this respect. You cannot give your doctor any specific instructions as to the sort of health care and life-sustaining medical care you want, but you can give instructions as to when you want your doctor to discontinue medical treatment.

# DEALING WITH DEATH

This chapter is not really written for you, but for your family and friends. What is the administrative red tape that must be unravelled when you die? How do your heirs get your estate? How does the administration of your estate work? What do they need to do? This chapter is written to help them, but if you understand what happens, you can prepare for that day. To help you prepare, we have prepared a short checklist at the end of this chapter

## WHAT TO DO WHEN SOMEONE DIES?

This section is a guide to what will happen when a person dies in Belgium. The section will explain the related administrative red tape and take you through the related process.

### Call a doctor

The first thing to do in case of death is to call a doctor, the family doctor or the doctor on call. He must confirm death and give you a medical certificate. If the person dies in a hospital, the staff will know what to do.

Usually, the body is not kept at home, a funeral parlour is better equipped to preserve the body and welcome visitors. The doctor will be able to advise you what arrangements to take to have the body taken to a funeral parlour (funerarium) or he will advise you to contact a funeral undertaker.

### The funeral undertaker

The funeral undertaker will deal with the administrative red tape: report the death, obtain the concession for burial or the authorisation for cremation and organise the funeral.

Check whether the deceased has not made an arrangement with a funeral undertaker to decide on funeral arrangements, to see if he has signed an insurance to cover the cost of his funeral or cremation, etc ...

www.funebra.be is the official website of Belgian funeral undertakers; you can easily find an undertaker close to you on this site. The site gives a few suggestions on dealing with the undertaker. Get a written quote with details of the expenses and do not let yourself be influenced by the emotions of the moment. A good suggestion is to make sure that you have a friend or a neighbour around who can be more objective. Always ask for a proper quote; do not accept a verbal quote or a quote on the back of an envelope. Do not pay an advance unless you have a quote with terms and conditions.

If your relative dies in hospital or a retirement home, you have no obligation to accept the undertaker proposed by the hospital or the home. If your relative died in a car accident or on the road, the police will normally ask a local funeral undertaker to take the body to a morgue or a private funeral home; he will send his bill to the authorities and you are not obliged to pay him or even use his services. You remain free to appoint your own funeral undertaker.

## Last wishes

Before you take any decisions about the funeral or cremation, check if there are no last wishes. Some people put their last wishes in their will and that is really where they should be. However, that may not be very practical. Sometimes it takes time before the will is found, in particular if it was left with a notary twenty years ago. Last wishes are best written out in a separate document.

If the deceased has left their body to science, the family should contact the hospital in question as soon as possible to make the arrangements to collect the body after the funeral, but within 48 hours. If you want to leave your body to science, you must clearly write that decision out in full, date and sign it; keep a copy and give a copy to the hospital. The hospital will usually give a card to keep with your identity card. The remains will be buried or cremated by the hospital; this can be months or years later. The cost is charged back to the family.

When you die in Belgium, the doctors may harvest your organs if you have been registered in the commune for more than six months. The law presumes that you agree to donate your organs; physicians may take your organs. However, they must check that you have not objected to organ donation.

If you do not want to donate your organs, you should not state this in your will. Organs must be taken immediately after death and it may take a while before your will is found and read. You have to make a statement in writing with the commune, a notary or a doctor. That will be noted in the national database of Belgian residents – the doctors must check that before taking organs.

## Reporting the death

The death must be reported at the registry office (*burgerlijke stand / état civil*) in the town hall. There is no time limit, but the sooner the better, because you will need an authorisation for the burial or cremation. The death must be reported by a relative, or by the funeral undertaker. These steps must be taken at the town hall of the commune where the deceased died (not where he was living at that time of death).

It is useful to bring the identity card and driver's licence of the deceased, the marriage book (*trouwboekje / livret de mariage*) together with the doctor's certificate.

The registry office will record the death. Copies of the death certificate will be provided so that the relatives can notify the death and to justify to their employers why they need some time off.

The spouse or partner and the children are entitled to three days off work with full pay, and so are the parents-in-law and the stepparents of the deceased. Siblings can take the day of the funeral off, but if they shared a house or apartment with the deceased, they can claim two days.

## Notifying the death

The first port of call is the adviser of the deceased, his lawyer or his notary, who can then start to check whether there is a will. They can also assist the heirs to release the bank accounts, to administer the estate, to file the inheritance tax return, and to distribute the assets.

There are a number of people and organisations that need to be notified of the death, preferably with a copy of the death certificate. The people who need to be notified are the employer, the accountant, the mutual insurance fund, the trade union, the insurance companies, the fund that pays out the family allowances, the pension authorities, the private pension funds and insurance companies that pay out a pension, the car registration office, etc.

Other parties to notify is the landlord, the tenants living in property of the deceased, the water company, the gas and electricity boards, etc ...

The bank must also be informed so that they can block the deceased's accounts.

The registry office will inform the tax authorities of your death; your family will then receive an invitation to file the inheritance tax return.

The widow or widower may be entitled to a pension if they are over 45 and had been married for a year. The application must be made via the town hall, within a year of the death.

# BANKS AND INSURANCE COMPANIES

The heirs must notify the death to all the banks where the deceased had an account. The bank will block all his accounts and cancel all debit and credit cards. All proxies given on the bank account cease upon death.

The bank blocks all bank accounts of a Belgian resident, even those he holds together with someone else (in particular their spouse, partner or registered partner). The personal bank accounts of their spouse are blocked as well, irrespective of whether they had community property. The partner and the registered partner of the deceased must not worry; their bank accounts will not get blocked.

There are two reasons why the bank blocks the accounts: to prevent any money being taking from the account and to allow the bank to report the bank account numbers and the balance on the day of death. In fact, it mostly protects the bank.

## How long are the accounts blocked?

That depends on the situation. If all your heirs live in the European Economic Area (the EEA is the European Union plus Iceland, Liechtenstein and Switzerland), the only obligation that banks and financial institutions have is to notify the tax authorities of the balance on the bank accounts before they release any money from these accounts. They just have to declare how much money is on the current and savings accounts and list the securities held on investment accounts.

The reason the banks block the accounts is so that they can be sure that they release the accounts to the rightful heirs. Before they release the bank accounts, the banks will require a certificate of succession. To make double sure that they cannot be held liable for releasing the bank accounts to the wrong people, the banks will also ask the heirs to sign a document confirming who can receive the money. Normally the accounts should be released in about two or three weeks, but if the heirs cannot agree amongst themselves, the account can remain frozen for a longer period of time.

The situation is more difficult if one of your heirs is living outside the EEA. In that case, the bank is obliged by law to freeze the account. The bank accounts remain blocked until the tax authorities deliver a certificate confirming that the inheritance tax has been paid or that sufficient guarantees have been given for the payment of the inheritance tax. Since the heirs have four months to file the tax return and another two to pay the tax, that can take some time.

## What does that mean?

The surviving spouse does not have access to either their own accounts or those of their spouse. In practice, the banks agree to pay the hospital and medical bills and the funeral bills. They will not, however, pay the rent, even if the deceased's salary or pension is paid into the account. Another problem can be that the shares and bonds owned by the deceased cannot be sold and reinvested.

The spouse or the civil partner can draw up to €5,000 from all the blocked accounts, with a maximum of half of the balance of the account. That is from the accounts they had together with the deceased and, from the personal accounts of their spouse. If they take out more than that, the excess is deducted from what they inherit.

However, that is something that should not be done lightly; the spouse who draws money from the account will be deemed to have accepted the inheritance, and once they accept the inheritance they are fair prey for the deceased's creditors (see p. 23). Taking out insurance may be a solution (see p.166).

## Bank safes

If there is a safe deposit box with a bank (even in joint names with someone else) the bank will seal the safe. The safe cannot be opened until there is a certificate of succession and the contents of the safe have been inventoried.

Opening the safe is an official procedure and the tax authorities must be invited. Unless the heirs can provide the key and the combination, a locksmith will have to open the safe. A detailed inventory is drawn up by the notary or a bank employee, and a copy is addressed to the tax authorities.

If one of your heirs lives outside the European Economic Area, the safe will be sealed again until the tax authorities deliver a certificate confirming that the inheritance tax has been paid or that sufficient guarantees have been given for the payment of the inheritance tax.

How do you find out where the deceased has a bank account or safe? You do not need to worry about addressing every possible bank. The Belgian Banking Federation offers a service to help locate these. A simple demand by the heirs, their lawyer or notary is sufficient, as long as if it comes with a death certificate and a certificate of succession showing that the heir is entitled to the content of the safe or bank account. The Federation charges €125 for the information and it passes the request to the banks that are a member of the federation. If there is an account or a safe the bank contacts the heirs directly.

## Insurance policies

Insurance companies established in Belgium have a legal obligation to notify the tax authorities of the existence of any insurance policies taken out by the deceased and/or his spouse to cover the value of any tangible movable assets; those can be the furniture, jewels, art, the car, etc. This gives the tax authorities an idea of the value of the estate.

## Certificate of succession

Before the banks release the bank accounts, they will request a certificate of succession (*attest van erfopvolging / certificat d'hérédité*) that states the identity of the deceased and of his heirs.

That certificate can be obtained from the tax collector in charge of inheritance tax. That can take a number of weeks because he needs to run a search on the Central Register of Wills.

In Belgium, the Central Register of Wills is kept by the Belgian Federation of Notaries; it arranges for the registration of a will in other countries and it answers all questions relating to the existence of a will or marriage contract, and where it can be found.

The Register can be contacted by the heirs if they present a death certificate (crt@fednot.be, tel. 02.505.08.11). The register can also check in Cyprus, Estonia, France, Italy, Lithuania, Luxembourg, the Netherlands, Portugal, Spain, Turkey and Ukraine.

When there is a will or a marriage contract that varies the normal order of succession, or if any of the heirs does not have the legal capacity to inherit (e.g. minors), a certificate will not be sufficient. In that case, a notary will have to analyse the will and the marriage contract and deduce from these who inherits what. He will draw up a deed of succession (*akte van erfopvolging / acte de notoriété*).

The notary or tax collector must first check that neither the deceased nor any of the beneficiaries has any tax or social security debts. When they are asked for a certificate or deed of succession, they must issue an enquiry and wait twelve working days. Only then can they deliver the certificate.

# ADMINISTRATION OF THE ESTATE

Belgium does not have a legal process comparable to probate for administering and distributing the property of a deceased person.

## No executor?

In Belgium, it is not necessary to appoint an executor or administrator to take possession of the estate and distribute it amongst the heirs and beneficiaries.

Even if a notary assists the heirs in the administration of the will, he is not the executor of the will or the administrator of the estate. The notary assists the heirs and beneficiaries with the liquidation of the estate, and even if he often is in the driving seat, he is not an executor.

Nevertheless, the deceased may appoint an executor in his will to ensure that the will is executed according to his will or that care is taken of non-financial provisions in a will. The powers of a Belgian executor are quite limited. Appointing a general legatee may be a good alternative.

## Administering the estate

The estate passes automatically from the deceased to the heirs of the deceased. For personal property, the heirs can just collect the belongings in the house and distribute them amongst themselves.

For money and shares in the bank they will have to provide a certificate or a deed of succession. The bank will transfer the money and the securities to the bank account of the heirs. For jewellery and valuables in the safe, they will hand them over after the inventory has been made and the banks are certain that all the heirs agree with the handover.

For real property, the transfer is recorded in the cadastre by the tax authorities when the inheritance tax return is processed. The cadastre is one of the three land registries in Belgium.

When the heirs have the assets in the estate, they are then responsible for administering the estate, paying debts, paying out bequests to legatees and distributing the assets in the estate.

## Opening the will

If the deceased has made bequests or given one heir more than another, he must draw up a will. It is only in movies that wills are read out by the family lawyer or the notary. That does not happen in real life, or not that I have witnessed.

If there is a will, the heirs are required to comply with it. If the deceased has left his car to a friend, the heirs must contact him to hand over the car. If they forget, the beneficiary must officially ask them for the handover of the car. If the heirs refuse, he has no alternative but to take them to court. Likewise any disputes between the heirs that cannot be solved amicably are decided by the court.

A notarised will has full effect and can be enforced without any further formal procedures. A handwritten will or an international will do not have the same effect. They have been written by the deceased and must be made official. When the heirs find a handwritten will, they must file it with a notary. If it is sealed, he will open it. He will draw up an official deed stating that he has received the will and describing the state of the will ("torn with three coffee stains").

The will is attached to that notarised deed. The notarised deed stays with the notary but a copy is lodged with the court of first instance so that it becomes as official as a notarised will. The procedure is the same for an international will.

However, the notary does not check whether the handwritten will has been written by the deceased. It is possible that the will is a fake, and any heir or beneficiary can contest the will. In that case, the heirs must prove that the will was drafted by the deceased and the court may ask a handwriting expert to confirm that. One way of contesting the will is by starting a criminal investigation, but that tends to delay the decision on the validity of the will; the will does indeed remain valid as long as no one has been condemned.

A foreign will witnessed by two witnesses is valid in Belgium, but it will have to be either lodged with a notary to be submitted to the court or recognised in court in the country where it was drafted.

## Do I have to accept the inheritance?

The heirs inherit an estate with all the assets of the deceased, but also with all his debts. They cannot be obliged to accept the estate. However, if they do not pay attention, they may be accepting the inheritance implicitly, e.g. if they remove some of the objects in the house, or if they ask the bank to pay them some money. In that case, they are taking on all the deceased's debts and liabilities.

## Can I refuse to inherit?

If you are an heir and you know that the deceased had more debts than liabilities, you can waive the inheritance. That must be done in a formal statement at the court of first instance.

If you are not sure what debts and liabilities you are taking on, there is another option. You can accept the inheritance on the condition that an inventory is first made of the estate, its assets and debts. You have three months to make a formal statement before the court of first instance and to get an inventory of assets and liabilities drawn up. You then have another 40 days to decide whether you accept the inheritance or not. That is the only way you can avoid being held liable for the debts of the deceased, but there may be nothing left in the estate.

## The inheritance tax return

If you inherit, your most important obligation is to file the inheritance tax return. The deadline is four months after the death if it occurs in Belgium, it is five months if the deceased died outside Belgium but in Europe, and six months if he died outside Europe. It is possible to obtain an extension from the tax office.

Filing the inheritance tax return is an obligation for the heirs and the general legatees. If the deceased has appointed an executor in his will, the executor may file the inheritance tax return, but he cannot be obliged to do so.

Each heir or legatee is liable for the inheritance tax on the share he receives in the inheritance. The inheritance tax is due two months after the end of the deadline for filing the inheritance tax return.

## WHAT IF THERE ARE YOUNG CHILDREN?

Parents are the guardian of their minor children (under the age of 18). There is no need to appoint a guardian when one parent dies. That is only necessary when both parents die. It is the justice of the peace (*vrederechter / juge de paix*) who appoints the guardian. In cross border situations, the justice of the peace may take interim measures for the protection of the children and of their assets.

If the deceased has appointed a guardian in his will or in an official statement before a notary or justice of the peace, the justice of the peace will normally appoint that person as the guardian. However, if the justice of the peace thinks that the proposed guardian is unsuitable or that appointing him would not to be in the best interests of the children, he can appoint someone else.

If the deceased has not appointed a guardian, the justice of the peace will appoint a guardian, usually a close family member. The justice of the peace will speak with children if they are over 12 and he will also speak with their brothers and sisters who are over 18, the grandparents, the uncles and aunts and anyone else who may wish to express an opinion.

The guardian must make an inventory of the estate of the child. He manages the property of the minor and he reports every year about the education of the child and his finances. However, the guardian (even the other parent is the guardian) needs the authorisation of the justice of the peace for major financial decisions such as the sale of property.

The justice of the peace will also appoint a supervisory guardian, preferably from the family of the other parent, who will report to him. The justice of the peace can also appoint two guardians, one who will look after the children and one who will be responsible for financial matters. Nobody can be obliged to act as a guardian or a supervisory guardian, and they can always ask to be released.

If a child has a dispute with the guardian, he can file a complaint with the public prosecutor's office if he is 12 (15 for money matters). A guardian who does not look after the best interests of the children can be revoked.

# CHECKLIST

- Do you want to leave your body to science?
  Contact the hospital and keep the card together with your identity card.

- Do you object to organ donation?
  Contact the commune, a notary or a doctor to stop organ donation.

- Do you have any specific requests for your funeral?
  Draw up your last wishes or get in touch with a funeral undertaker to make the arrangements for your funeral (burial, cremation, ...)

- Do you want to take out insurance to cover the cost of your funeral?
  Contact an insurance company, a funeral insurance company (look up *"uitvaartverzekering"* or *"assurance obsequies"*).

- Make arrangements for your spouse so that they have access to money when the accounts are blocked, or take out insurance to provide funds.

- Make a will, consider if you will need an executor of the will.
  If you have made a will, leave a note so that your relatives can locate it.

- If you have young children, make a formal statement to appoint a guardian.

- Make a personal checklist to help your heirs and beneficiaries locate the people they need to notify, the contracts they need to terminate, your bank accounts and assets, your debts and liabilities, etc...

# WHO INHERITS WHAT ?

The answer to this question depends on whether or not you made a will. If you make a will, you can decide who gets what. However, if you do not make a will, your estate does not just go to the State.

There is a set of rules in the law that explains who gets what if you die without a will, if your will is not valid, or if it does not deal with certain questions.

If you are domiciled in Belgium, who inherits what depends on what you have in your estate and on who you leave behind.

## WHAT IS IN YOUR ESTATE?

Your estate includes all your property: that is the real property you own in Belgium or abroad, any movables such as clothing, jewellery, furniture, artwork, cash, cars, money on your bank accounts, shares and bonds, etc... minus any debts and liabilities you have at the time of your death.

If you are married and you have community property, normally half of that community property belongs to you and will fall in your estate to be inherited by your heirs; the other half belongs to your spouse. However, in your marriage contract you may have given more than half of the community property to your spouse.

If you own a share in a property (co-ownership), e.g. a house that you bought or inherited with one or more other people, only that share is in your estate.

What is also in your estate is any income to which you were entitled up to the day of death.

Moreover, if you have taken out an insurance policy but not appointed a beneficiary, the insurance company will pay out the insured capital to your estate.

## What is not in your estate?

If you have the usufruct of a house or an apartment, that usufruct dies with you. It is a temporary right to live in a house or apartment, or to rent it out, but when you die, you cannot give it to someone else.

If you have taken out insurance, the insured capital is, in principle, not part of your estate. The beneficiary can claim the payment directly from the insurance company without having to ask your heirs.

## Debts and liabilities

From the value of the estate, we deduct all the personal debts of the deceased and half of the debts of the community property, the funeral and final expenses such as hospital fees.

If the debts and liabilities exceed the value of the estate, the heirs should waive the estate or ask for an inventory of the assets and liabilities.

# WHO DO YOU LEAVE BEHIND ?

## Children but no spouse or partner

Let us start with a common situation; you are survived by your children or grandchildren, but your spouse or partner has died before you or you have divorced.

If you have not divorced but live separately, your spouse will still inherit (see p. 30)

For most of us, our heirs are our children and they get your entire estate; they must share. How they do that is their business, but the rule is that they get an equal share. A child that has died before you does not inherit; your estate is then divided between the other children, unless he has children of his own.

### Children

Children from a previous relationship or marriage inherit from you. They remain your children even if you and their mother or father are not married anymore or have never been married.

Illegitimate children inherit as well; children do not need to be legitimate to inherit. Children born to parents who are not married to each other inherit in the same way as children of a married couple. A child that is not recognised by the father can inherit in the same way as a recognised child, if he or she files a successful paternity suit.

That was the reason that French-Italian actor Yves Montand was ex-humed six years after his death. The DNA sample that he had refused during his life was taken from his remains, but it did not prove the actor was the father.

Children that are not born when their father dies can inherit if they are born within 300 days after their father's death. In the Belgian civil code, children are conceived between 180 and 300 days before their birth. That would mean that a child that is conceived through IVF years after the death of the father could not inherit.

### Grandchildren

Grandchildren do not inherit directly from their grandparents unless their parent has died and then they take his or her place as heirs. One of your children can chose to let your inheritance skip a generation. It is their decision, and all they need to do is waive the inheritance in favour of their children. Generation skipping can save on inheritance tax: inheritance tax is not due on the transfer from the first to the second generation, but from the second to the third.

If grandchildren inherit in the place of their parent, they do not get an equal share as their uncles and aunts. Together they receive the share their parent would have received, and they share that in equal shares.

E.g.    *If you have three children, they receive a third each. If your daughter Betty died before you, her two children inherit the share she would have received and receive a sixth each.*

### Stepchildren

The children of your spouse or partner do not inherit from you, and the children you had from a previous relationship do not inherit from your spouse or partner. Stepchildren do not inherit from their stepparents because they are not blood relatives even if they have lived their entire life with the family.

Stepchildren can inherit if you provide for them in your will, but in that case you need to make sure that your own children receive at least what they are entitled to under the forced heirship rules. Please note that stepchildren are already assimilated to children for inheritance tax purposes.

### Adopted children

Adopted children inherit in the same way as biological children. Belgium has two types of adoption; ordinary adoption and full adoption. While full adoption definitively cuts the ties between the child and the biological parent, ordinary adoption does not. In that case, the child inherits from his biological as well as from his adoptive parents.

# You leave children and a spouse or partner

When you are survived by your children and your spouse or partner, your children inherit your entire estate in equal shares, but your spouse inherits the usufruct on your estate. We will explain usufruct in another chapter, but in general terms, having the usufruct means that you have the right to live in a house, or let it out and receive the income from the investments and savings, but someone else is the owner.

### Children

All your children inherit bare ownership; the children you have together with your spouse, the children you have from a previous marriage or relationship or even outside a relationship, children that you have recognised and those that you have not, even a child born less than 300 days after the father's death (see above).

Grandchildren can take the place of their parents.

All your children inherit from you but they only inherit bare ownership. If you and your spouse are in one of these situations, you should read the next chapter on usufruct because your spouse and your children may have a conflict.

### Spouse

Only your spouse inherits the usufruct on your entire estate, even a spouse in a same sex marriage. Belgium allows same sex marriages - and recognises foreign same sex marriages - and if your husband survives you, he inherits the usufruct as well, while your children from a previous relationship become the owners of your estate.

It does not matter that your spouse is not the father or mother of your children, or even that he or she is the same age as your children.

When you divorce, your ex is not your spouse anymore and does not inherit from you. However, if you have separated without divorcing, he or she still is your spouse and inherits the usufruct just as if you were still living together.

The difference is that if you have been separated for at least six months, you can disinherit your spouse in your will. That will only have effect if you had asked the court to authorise your separation. If you part ways and sign your husband out of your will, but do not live for another six months after the separation, the will is not going to have any effect and he will inherit anyway. Moreover, if you reunite with your spouse and he has moved back in, your will will be disregarded and your spouse will inherit.

### A partner is not a spouse

When you have children, and you are survived by a partner, your children inherit everything, even if your partner is their mother or father. The only way to make sure that your partner inherits from you is to make a provision in your will or to register your partnership.

In Belgium, partners can register their partnership (*wettelijke samenwoning / cohabitation légale*). A registered partnership is similar to a civil partnership in the U.K., or a PACS in France. To register your partnership, you have to sign a statement at the town hall of the commune where they live. The registered partnership creates certain rights and obligations, but it can be terminated more easily than a marriage. It ends when one partner dies, marries or demands a termination.

Registered partners do not inherit like spouses. Registered partners only inherit the usufruct of the family home and the usufruct of the furniture and furnishings in the family home owned by their partner. All the rest is inherited by his children: the bare ownership of the family home and of the content, but in particular their partner's personal property and savings (in full ownership!). They will ultimately be able to sell the house and the contents and the deceased partner's personal property.

Registered partners who owned the family home and the furniture together may find that they own that together with their partner's children and that they will have to buy them out.

Registered partners need to make a will if they want to give each other more security. On the other hand, if they fall out, it is easy to change one's will to deny one's partner the usufruct on the family home and the contents.

# You leave a spouse or partner, no children

You are married or in a relationship but you have no children or grandchildren; the children of your spouse or partner, your stepchildren do not count. In this case, your spouse or partner will inherit from you, together with your family.

### The rights of the widow(er)

If the deceased does not leave any children, the widow(er) receives all the community property but only the usufruct of the separate property of the deceased. We will explain the difference between community property and separate property in another chapter (see p. 65).

For most Belgian couples, the family assets are community property; they own them together and half of the community property falls in their estate. They also have separate property; that is what they owned before their marriage, or what they inherited or received from their family.

Usually, the personal estate of either spouse is minimal. If the deceased has no children, the surviving spouse gets everything, or almost everything.

If there is no community property, because the couple has signed a marriage contract or because they are a couple from a common law country that does not have community property, they may find out that they only inherit the usufruct of the family assets which are owned by their spouse. They only have the right to use the family assets for the rest of their lives, but the assets are owned by the family of their spouses.

When they die, their in-laws will get it all. These may not be able to access anything until the widow(er) dies, but they can stop the surviving spouse from selling the assets.

32

There will be nothing for the surviving spouse to leave to his or her own nieces and nephews.

It is only when no heirs can be found, that the surviving spouse inherits everything.

### You are separated

An ex-spouse does not inherit, but as long as a married couple is not divorced, they can inherit from each other. Even when they are in the process of getting a divorce, they still inherit from each other, but they can draw up a will to prevent this. As long as they do not start living together again, they can disinherit their spouse. The only condition is that they live for another six months and had not opposed the court decision allowing the couple to live separately.

### You have not married your partner

A partner does not inherit; you have to draw up a will to appoint your partner as your beneficiary in your will or register your partnership.

The law does not give registered partners the same rights as a spouse; they are only entitled to the usufruct of the family home and the usufruct of the furniture and furnishings in that family home that belonged to their partner. Their partner's relatives will inherit all the rest: the bare ownership of the family home, the bare ownership of the content, but most importantly the full ownership of his or her personal property and savings.

If registered partners owned the family home and the furniture together, they own half and they inherit the usufruct on their partner's half. They may have to buy out their partner's family.

When no heirs can be found, the surviving partner still only inherits the usufruct of the family home and the content, while the Belgian State may inherit all the rest. A spouse would inherit the entire estate.

The only way to give your registered partner more security is by drawing up a will. That is the only solution for non-registered partners. If you live with someone who has promised you something in his will, keep in mind that a will can always be retracted. Even a registered partner can be left with nothing at all.

## You leave no spouse, no partner, no children

If you have no children or grandchildren, and you have no partner or spouse, we need to look a bit further away from home to find your heirs. However, that means that you can freely choose who will get everything by drawing up a will.

If you have not had a chance to do that, if the will is not found or is invalid, there is a set of rules that explain who gets what.

The first group of heirs are your parents and siblings. Your parents inherit together with your brothers and sisters, half-brothers and half-sisters (and their children, i.e. your nieces and nephews). Each parent receives one quarter. The rest is then distributed between your brothers and sisters.

If you have no siblings, your ascendants inherit everything. Your ascendants are your parents, your grandparents and your great-grandparents. Half of your estate goes to your mother's side of the family and the other half to your father's side. If your ascendants have died before you, someone, usually the notary will look for their descendants.

If you have none of the above, your estate is inherited by your parents' brothers and sisters, your uncles and aunts and their children, or even a step further, your great-uncles and great-aunts and their children. Again half goes to each side of the family. These heirs are your blood relatives: uncles and aunts by marriage do not inherit.

Finally, if you really do not have any heirs and no surviving spouse or partner, the entire estate goes to the Belgian State. That is not as uncommon as you would think in these days with families migrating all over the world losing contact in the process.

# LAST WILL AND TESTAMENT

In the previous chapter, we looked at the rules that apply when you do not make a will. These are the default rules and you can make a will to change these. In this chapter we will see how you make a will, what you can do with a will and, more importantly, what you cannot do with a will.

## DO I NEED A WILL IN BELGIUM?

No, you do not need a Belgian will if you are happy with the Belgian default solution (the children receive the bare ownership and the surviving parent the usufruct). However, a will may be useful to make certain specific provisions.

### Why would I need a will in Belgium?

There are different reasons why you might want to draw up a will.

The first reason is to decide who gets what. You can make specific bequests. You can decide that your son will get your collection of watches and that your daughter will get her mother's jewellery and you can leave small sums of money to some friends or relatives. You can also decide that one of the children receives more, e.g. if they have more difficulties building up a successful professional career or may need a hand e.g. to buy a first house.

Keep in mind that you cannot disinherit certain heirs, like your children or your spouse (see p. 49).

If you anticipate that one of your children is going to make difficulties for your wife, you can deny your heirs the right to ask for the conversion or capitalisation of that usufruct (see p. 63). You can also give her the maximum you are allowed to give to her so that she can keep more control over more assets.

You can also use a will to attach conditions to a bequest. You can use that to make sure someone gets something, but you can also do this to make a bequest more tax efficient.

Finally, you can make a will to reduce the inheritance tax.

These are all forms of estate planning; we will go into more detail in the chapter "Planning your will" where we will see how you can make a will to plan your estate and to make it more tax efficient (see p. 116).

## Other uses of wills

A will must not only deal with your belongings and your estate.

### Funeral arrangements

In your will, you can decide what sort of funeral ceremony you want and what music you want, you may want to have a message read or you may want to give instructions for the funeral eulogy.

You can decide that you want to be buried or cremated, where you want that to happen, whether you want remembrance Masses to be said, etc.

### Donate your organs

If you want to donate your body to science, you should not do that in your will. The hospital needs to be warned in advance. It may take weeks before your will is found. That is also the reason why you should not only put in your will that you do not want to donate your organs; they may have been collected (see p. 16).

### Appoint a guardian for young children

A will can also be used to appoint a guardian for under age orphans if both their parents have died (see p. 24). You can also make a statement before a notary or a justice of the peace. The justice of the peace is then obliged to appoint that person as the guardian unless that person has become unsuitable, or refuses to be appointed.

When you appoint a guardian, you have to provide appropriate information. For the children, that is their names, place and date of birth and an explanation of the current custody arrangement in particular when the parents are separated. For the guardian, you should also mention their address and phone numbers and if they are a relative, their relationship to the child.

Do not forget your own details and those of the other parent (name, place and date of birth, address and phone numbers). Keep in mind that unless you have sole custody of your child, you need the other parent's consent. Include a statement confirming that both parents consent to the guardianship and understand the implications of their decision.

If you make any other written statement to appoint a guardian, try to do it in the form of a codicil to your will. You cannot make a will together with the other parent, not even when you are married. We suggest that both parents make the same guardianship papers and mention that in the papers.

If you make a single document signed by both parents that would not necessarily be a valid appointment of a guardian, but if it is clear that that was what you wanted. The justice of the peace will normally appoint the person you have chosen.

### Appoint an executor

Although Belgian law does not require an executor to administer and liquidate the estate of the deceased, you can appoint an executor in your will. If not, you leave it to your heirs to execute the will and to the beneficiaries to check that they have done it properly. Any problems and disputes will then be sorted out in court.

In Belgium, heirs automatically inherit the deceased's estate. An executor is not needed to enter into possession of any assets in order to distribute them to the heirs and legatees.

If you appoint an executor in your will (*testamentuitvoerder / exécuteur testamentaire*), he is your representative and he ensures that your will is executed in accordance with your wishes. His powers are limited. He does not have any powers to oblige your heirs to do what you want. He can take precautionary measures (have the house sealed off, make an inventory, ...), but he can only oblige your heirs to pay the legacies by taking them to court.

He does not have any powers to distribute and give out the assets of the deceased, or sell them. The deceased may state in his will that the executor will have possession, but only of moveable assets, never of real property. An executor with possession can collect receivables, pay off your debts and pay out legacies.

Possession ends after one year and one day. On that day the executor must present the accounts of his management of the estate. This allows the executor to pay off debtors and pay out legacies. Possession can only be granted for a period of one year and one day.

An executor may prove useful to take care of non-financial provisions in a will.

## Other provisions

Some people use their will to give their family and friends some philosophical considerations or thoughts or more practical information for their next of kin.

Do not expect that this will has much effect or that your will can be enforced. George Orwell's will requested that no biography of him be written; that did not stop the production of many biographies, in particular in the year 1984.

You may also want to decide what happens to your Facebook or LinkedIn profile. Do you want to have it deleted or keep it as a remembrance page?

# HOW DO I MAKE A VALID WILL?

Belgium accepts three types of will. You can write your own will, you can type it up, put in an envelope and lodge it with a notary, or you can ask a notary to prepare a will. Even if you are not Belgian, you can draw up your will in any of these forms and if you have a foreign will, that will normally be valid as well, but a foreign will can always raise concerns.

## A handwritten will

The handwritten will is the easiest and cheapest way of drafting a will. You take a pen and a piece of paper and you start writing. A spoken will recorded on a DVD or in a video message is not valid.

You just have to make sure that it is completely written out in longhand, dated and signed. Make sure that nobody adds anything and that the date is written out in full. And finally, use your normal signature. A handwritten will does not need to be witnessed.

It is preferable to draw up a will in Dutch or French depending on where in Belgium you live. That avoids the cost of translating it later. An example (in English) can be found in the annexes.

# An international will

The international will is called so because it was introduced by the Washington Convention of 1973 introducing a uniform law for international wills. It is international in that it may be drawn up in any language, and is enforceable in all countries that ratified the convention. Those countries are Bosnia and Herzegovina, Canada, Cyprus, Ecuador, France, Italy, Libya, Niger, Portugal, Slovenia and Yugoslavia.

The international testament is a handwritten or even typed document that you present in an envelope to a notary. It may even have been written or typed by someone else and it may be drafted in any language.

You add the date and sign the will in front of the notary who then draws up a deed in which he notes that you have stated that the document is your will and that you know the content.

That deed is witnessed by two witnesses; you do not need to bring your own witnesses, the notary usually has some people he can call in. You do not need to tell the notary or the witnesses what is in the will. The notary does not read the will or check that it is valid. The notary finally records the existence of the will with the Central Register for Wills.

# The notarised will

The notarised will is drafted by a notary who writes it as you dictate it, even in a foreign language. The notary simply translates your last wishes into one of the three Belgian official languages (Dutch, French or German).

That is the theory, what happens is that you have a first meeting with the notary where you tell him what you want in your will and what you want to leave to whom. The notary prepares a draft that he sends to you to review.

If that draft suits you, you make another appointment, the notary reads the will, you sign it with the notary and two witnesses provided by the notary.

The major advantage of a notarised will is that the notary will make sure that it is correctly drafted and that it is valid. A notarised will is not free; it costs about €200 to 300. You cannot keep the content of your will hidden from the notary and the witnesses but they are not allowed to reveal the content of your will. That is why nobody else can attend your meeting with the notary.

The notarised will is registered with the Central Register of Wills. A simple search with that register will show with which notary you have made a will, in Belgium or in one of the few countries that have a scheme for the registration of wills. Currently these are Belgium, Cyprus, Estonia, France, Italy, Lithuania, Luxembourg, the Netherlands, Portugal, Spain, Turkey and Ukraine.

It is also very difficult to contest a notarised will, since the notary is a public officer. To have it declared null and void, one would have to prove that the notarised will has been forged.

## A foreign will?

If you have made a will outside Belgium, that will be recognised in Belgium as a valid will, if it was drafted in your country of nationality, of domicile or residence, or even under the rules of the country where you own real estate.

The will must comply with the law of that country but it must also comply with certain basic conditions of Belgian law; if not it could be disregarded. There are a few definite exclusions: you cannot make a will together with your spouse and you cannot make a will together where you leave everything to each other. Two separate wills in which you leave everything to each other are valid. Setting up a trust by will creates another set of problems (see p. 186).

The major problem with foreign wills is that they do not take account of the limitations described below and in particular the forced heirship rules (see p. 49).

## What is the most appropriate form of will?

First of all you do not need to be a Belgian to draft a handwritten will or an international or notarised will.

The handwritten will has a lot of advantages. It can be drafted without any formalities and it is free, so that it has become the most popular form of will. It remains secret and you can always tear it up. It is the most adequate form in emergency situations, e.g. just before you go on holiday. If you want to change your will frequently a handwritten will is easier than regular visits to the notary.

However, there are as many disadvantages. If you make your will on your own, you may make a mistake on the form or you may be badly advised on what the law says. Any mistakes can lead to protracted litigation in court. That can also happen with an international will: you write or type it and give it to a notary for safekeeping. The notary does not reviewing the content of the will.

The best place to keep a handwritten will is somewhere safe at home on in your safe. However, there will always be the risk that it is never discovered, that it gets lost, or thrown out by accident, or that the finder feels that he has more to gain if it never surfaces. Whoever finds a handwritten will must give it to a notary to make it official and he must not hold it back. That could what happens if it falls in the wrong hands.

If that worries you, you can leave your handwritten will with a notary. The notary will then record the will with the Central Register of Wills, just like an international or a notarised will. The will remains secret; the register does not have the content of the will, just the name of the person who has made a will and the notary and the date. Upon death, the notary will do a search with the register and he will receive a list with all the references of notaries where a will or a change to the marriage contract has been registered. Those wills cannot go missing.

A handwritten will is free but when it is registered with the notary there will be a cost of €50. For a notarised will or an international will, the notary will charge you €250 (he has to pay the witnesses).

It is also easier to contest a handwritten will. People who feel hard done by may want to prove that the date is not correct, that you were not sound of mind when you drew up your will, they may challenge that it is your signature or handwriting, and ask for a graphology test. That cannot happen to a will that is notarised; the notary and the witnesses have heard you declare that this is your will.

The major hurdle for a foreign will is that each country has its legal system and its own ways of drawing up a will. In some countries, you can leave your estate to your Chihuahua or your cat; that would be invalid in Belgium. A joint will, e.g. between husband and wife, in one single document is not valid, and neither are is a mutually binding will so that upon the first death, the surviving spouse is not free to dispose of his or her property.

Mirroring wills are allowed. These are two separate, identical wills, e.g. leaving everything to each other. Of course, I must repeat that disinheriting your children is definitely not an option.

## LEGATEES

An heir is someone who succeeds to your entire estate, the person who inherits when there is no will. The person named in a will is a legatee. There is quite a difference between inheriting as an heir or as a legatee, and then there are different sorts of legatees.

A legatee can be named to receive a particular asset of the estate or a fixed sum of money – what is generally understood to be a legacy. If you leave a car or €100,000 to a legatee, he will have to ask the heirs to hand over the car or the money. If you have two children, that should not be too difficult. They will administer the estate and give the legatee what he is entitled to.

If, however, you have no direct relatives, and you leave your car or money to a friend, the notary will have to find all your heirs. They may be cousins twice removed in the States and in Eastern Europe with cousin Sheldon in Hong Kong. The notary will have to get them all to agree, give a proxy to administer the estate and pay out the bequest.

In that situation, it makes sense to appoint a general legatee (*algemeen legataris/ légataire universel*). That is someone to whom the testator leaves his entire estate. There is no standard wording to appoint a general legatee; the following is perfectly valid: *"I leave all my possessions to … whom I appoint as my general legatee"*, but *"and the rest of my estate will go to …"* will do as well. The legacy of the usufruct over the entire estate or the legacy of the bare ownership of the entire estate is a general legacy as well.

All the rights to the estate are automatically transferred to the general legatee; contrary to other (specific) legatees, he does not have to petition the heirs or general legatees to receive his bequest.

The general legatee receives the entire estate of the deceased, or what is left after he has paid out the legacies. Of course, if the testator has forced heirs, they will receive the share they must receive, and what the general legatee receives will be limited to the disposable part.

Appointing a general legatee sounds good but it comes with a set of obligations as well as privileges. As a general legatee, he can and must administer the estate.

That means he must pay off the debts of the deceased.

It is also the general legatee who has to carry out the bequests (hand over the Picasso, the 15 year old Jaguar, or the deceased's cherished chair). It can also help with the administration of the estate. If there is no general legatee, other legatees will have to ask the family, and the heirs may be loathsome to do this when they have been partially disinherited in the will.

The general legatee has to file the inheritance tax return. Normally, that is an obligation for the heirs. Other legatees can only be obliged to file a tax return for what they received from the estate when the heirs and the general legatees fail to comply with their obligation.

Finally, being a general legatee carries some risks as well. While each heir or legatee must pay inheritance tax on his share in the estate, heirs and general legatees can be made to pay the inheritance tax due by other beneficiaries.

# LIMITS TO THE FREEDOM OF MAKING WILLS

By making a will, you can give more to one heir than to another and you can also leave assets for another person who would otherwise not inherit. However, the freedom to dispose of your belongings by will is not unlimited.

## Who can make a will?

To make a valid will, you need to be over 18 and "of sound mind", in other words you need to be mentally fit. Minors over 16 may make a will for half their assets; minors under the age of 16 cannot make a will. People who are mentally ill, senile, or suffering from some other debility cannot make a will if they have been declared legally incompetent by a court decision.

If you have been declared bankrupt, you can no longer dispose of your assets in a will. If you draw up a will, it will only be executed after your debtors have been paid.

## Who cannot be the beneficiary in a will?

Everyone can be a beneficiary. You can make a will in favour of a minor or someone who has been declared legally incompetent. Of course, the beneficiary also needs to have the capacity to accept the legacy. If that is not the case, his parents or guardian will have to accept the legacy. The beneficiaries become the owners but their parents or guardians manage the property.

You can even leave something to an unborn child as long as it is conceived before your death if it is born after your death.

## Community property

Spouses can only include and dispose by will of their part of the community property. If a spouse wishes to dispose of a specific asset that is community property, this asset will only be passed on to the beneficiary if it falls in the estate of the deceased. If not, the beneficiary can only claim the countervalue of the specific asset from the heirs.

Spouses can freely dispose of their separate property, as long as they abide with the forced heirship rules.

## Substitution

Finally, also forbidden is "substitution" (or *fideicommissio*). That is a bequest in a will where one leaves something for a first beneficiary with the obligation to keep it for – and pass it on to – a second beneficiary you name in your will. Substitution is, however authorised in two specific situations: a bequest to a child with the obligation to pass the asset on to their living or future children, and a bequest to a brother or sister with the obligation to keep it for their children.

## The forced heirship rules

When drafting a will, one has to take account of the so-called forced heirship rules. We will deal with that in a separate chapter.

# Revoking a will

A will can be revoked at any time.

That can be done by an express declaration in a notarised deed or in a new will e.g. *"I revoke any other last wills and testaments which I may have made in the past"*. It does not even need to be made in the same form; a notarised will can be revoked by a handwritten will.

You can also revoke your will implicitly. You can make a new will that contradicts the content of the first will.

*E.g.* *If you left your Picasso to Johnny in your first will, you can invalidate that by leaving it to Henry in a later will.*

And if you sell the Picasso that you had left to Johnny, there will not be a Picasso left in your estate for Johnny. There is nothing Johnny can do about it; he cannot get any compensation for your change of mind.

# FORCED HEIRSHIP

In Belgium, you must give a part of your estate to certain relatives. The law reserves a part of your estate to your children, your spouse and sometimes your parents. That is the "reserved portion" or the "forced estate". These rules are obligatory. Hence the name "forced heirship rules".

## WHY?

Forced heirship rules are typical of Civil law systems that do not recognize total freedom of testation. They can be traced back to a Germanic custom for intestate inheritance. The personal property of the deceased (that is everything that is not real property) was divided into thirds - the widow's part, the bairn's part (the *legitime*) and the dead's part. This part consisted of his clothes, weapons, farm animals and implements that were usually buried with the deceased. In time, with the revival of the will, the dead's part came to be freely disposable.

## WHO AND HOW MUCH?

The forced estate is reserved for the forced heirs listed in the law; the law also determines what share they are entitled to. In Belgium, these forced heirs are the children, your spouse and your parents. The following schedule summarises what each forced heir must get as a minimum and how much you are free to leave to whoever you want.

| Heir | Forced part | Disposable part |
|---|---|---|
| Children | | |
| 1 child | 1/2 of estate | 1/2 of estate |
| 2 children | 2/3 of estate | 1/3 of estate |
| 3 children | 3/4 of estate | 1/4 of estate |
| 4 or more | 3/4 of estate | 1/4 of estate |
| Spouse | Usufruct of 1/2 of estate or Usufruct of the family home | Bare ownership of 1/2 of estate + full ownership of 1/2 of estate |
| Parents | | |
| 1 parent | 1/4 of estate | 3/4 of estate |
| 2 parents | 1/2 of estate | 1/2 of estate |

These forced heirship rules are obligatory. That means you cannot disinherit your forced heirs, even if they are under age or incapable of taking care of their person or administering their estates because of mental incapacity or physical infirmity.

## FORCED HEIRSHIP IN PRACTICE

If you have no children, spouse or parents, you can leave everything to whoever you want. If you have forced heirs, they limit your freedom to make a will.

## The children

If there is only one child, that child must receive at least half of his or her parents' assets. Two thirds are reserved if there are two children, and if there are three or more children, three quarters are reserved for them. All children are protected: recognised and non-recognised children, adopted children, children from a previous marriage or relationship (see p. 28).

Grandchildren can be entitled to a forced share as well but only if their parent, who would have been the forced heir, has died first. They take their parent's place as forced heirs and they are entitled to the forced portion their parent would have been entitled to. That means that when a grandmother wants to make a bequest directly to her grandchildren, she must take account of the forced portion of her own children.

If she has two children and two grandchildren, she cannot give her grandchildren more than a third of her estate in her will or during her lifetime. If she gives them more, her children could get the will reduced or the donation undone.

## The parents

The parents of the deceased (or even his grandparents) may be forced heirs as well, but only if the deceased does not have any children.

Each parent can claim a quarter of the estate. If one parent has died, the right to the forced portion passes to the grandparents. The grandparents on the mother's side can claim one quarter and the grandparents on the father's side can claim another quarter.

The law will be changed, most likely in order to do away with this forced heirship rule. In the meantime, you can disinherit your parents and grandparents with a provision in your will in favour of your spouse. If the parents are needy, they can claim maintenance from the estate of their child, but that is limited to what would have been their forced share.

# The surviving spouse

The surviving spouse is entitled to a forced portion as well. The spouse must receive at least either the usufruct over half the estate of the deceased or the usufruct in the family home and the furniture and contents of the family home. The spouse has the choice. He or she cannot waive that right, except if she marries someone who has children from a previous marriage or relationship (see p. 159).

When one is survived by a spouse and other forced heirs, we have to combine the rules for both.

### A surviving spouse and children

If one has two or more children and a surviving spouse, there appears to be an inconsistency between the intestacy rules (if there is no will, the surviving spouse inherits the usufruct over the entire estate of the deceased) and the forced heirship rules (if there is a will, the surviving spouse must inherit at least the usufruct over half of the estate of the deceased).

The answer is simple when you think about it. When you do nothing, your spouse inherits the usufruct over your estate, and your children inherit the bare ownership of your estate, but you can leave less for your spouse, since he/she must only receive (at least) the usufruct over half your estate.

The question then is what you want to do.

If you want to leave your spouse as much as possible you can leave your children only the bare ownership of half, a third or a quarter of your estate.

If you have one child, your spouse can get the full ownership of half your estate and the usufruct over the other half.

If you have two children, you are free to leave your spouse the full ownership of one third of your estate and the usufruct over two thirds.

And if you have three or more children, your spouse can receive the full ownership of one quarter of your estate and the usufruct over three quarters of your estate.

If, on the contrary, you want to leave your spouse the minimum, that would be just the usufruct over half your estate. That usufruct is then taken on both the forced and the disposable portion of your estate.

A single child must receive the full ownership of one quarter of your estate and the usufruct over another quarter. The disposable part is then still half of your estate: the full ownership of one quarter of your estate and the usufruct over another quarter.

Two children receive the full ownership of one third of your estate and the usufruct over another third. The disposable part is a third, i.e. a sixth in full ownership and a sixth in usufruct.

And if you have three or more children, they must get at least the full ownership of three eights of your estate, and the usufruct over another three eights.

### A surviving spouse and parents

If one is survived by one's spouse and one or both parents, the forced share for both can be combined. The usufruct of the spouse on half of the estate will apply to the quarter that is reserved for each parent; instead of a quarter in full ownership, they can claim an eight in full ownership and an eight in bare ownership.

Two parents are entitled to half of the estate, and the usufruct on the other half must be inherited by the spouse. In that case one is free to leave the bare ownership of that half to anyone else.

If there is one parent, the reserve is only one quarter, so that one can dispose of the bare ownership of half and the full ownership of a quarter.

# WHAT IF YOU GIVE AWAY TOO MUCH?

When you have forced heirs, you always have a disposable portion of your estate that you can give away to anyone you like: your children, your wife, your parents or anyone else in your will or through lifetime gifts.

If you have given away too much during your lifetime, or if you are being too generous in your will, only your heirs can do something about it. They can refuse to hand over bequests, they can claim back donations or they can ask the judge to intervene. Nobody else (not even the taxman) can do that in their place. If they do nothing, and they acknowledge what you wanted to do, nobody can do anything about it.

How does this work in practice ?

## Reconstitute the estate

To determine what your forced heirs are entitled to and what you are free to give away, we have to reconstitute your entire estate on a piece of paper or in a spread sheet.

We take the value of your estate left at the time of your death, deduct the debts and liabilities, add anything that has been given away during your lifetime and calculate the maximum disposable portion from there.

## Add lifetime donations

All donations must be added to the value of your estate ... on paper. That does not mean that everyone who has received anything must bring it back immediately. All donations must be accounted for, but not all donations will be cancelled.

In that respect, it does not make any difference when and how the gift was made: before a notary, by way of hand to hand donation or by a transfer from one bank account to another. One donation is not safer than another.

Even donations made more than three years before the death of the donor must be added. The famous three years rule is a rule of inheritance tax law (see p. 65). It means that donations made less than three years before the death of the donor are liable to inheritance tax while donations made more than three years before are not.

There are a few exceptions; a donation of goods where you retain the usufruct or a donation against an annuity to one of your heirs is not added to your estate provided that the other heirs agreed to that donation.

Donations in a marriage contract are not taken into account as donations. That means that one can get around the forced heirship rules and disinherit children of the couple by leaving everything to each other in a marriage contract (see p. 156).

Finally, financial help to your children does not constitute a donation. Paying for your son's university studies in the States, at a cost of €100,000 is not a donation but the financial support which you owe to your children. Giving your daughter €100,000 to start a new business is a donation. Your daughter's €100,000 may have to be added to your estate while the cost of the studies in the States may not.

## The value of these donations

This section is rather technical, and related legal advice will be necessary, but we need to draw your attention to this.

All assets left in the estate are appraised for the value they have on the day of the deceased's death.

That is also the case for past donations. That is logical, because they are deemed to be still in his estate on that day. However, the consequences can be harsh.

If the market drops two months after the day of his death and stocks become penny stocks, that is bad luck. We need to look at the value on the day of death. If shares donated drop in value before his death, that is lucky for the person who has received the shares.

However, what happens usually is that donations gain in value.

E.g.    if a father gives his son a piece of land worth €100,000, and that land is worth €200,000 at the time of the father's death, the donation will be added to the father's estate for €200,000. If he had given cash for €100,000 that cash would still be counted for €100,000.

What is more appalling is the situation of the father who gives the shares of his company to the son who takes over the business, the company gains a lot of value due to the son's hard work, and triples in value. If he had given his daughter an equivalent amount of cash, that would not have changed in value. On the day of the reckoning, the son may have to compensate his sister. A donation-division may be a solution for this problem.

## Determine the disposable part

When donations are added to the value of the estate, we can determine the disposable part. This must be compared to the donations made by the deceased and the bequests he wanted to make in his will. If the disposable part of the estate is larger, then there is no problem. It is only if the donations and bequests in an estate exceed the disposable part that they must be reduced. Reductions are made in the following ways:

### Bequests are reduced

The bequests in the will are reduced first. Any bequests in a will that impinge on the disposable estate are partially cancelled so that the heirs receive the share that is reserved for them. The heirs cannot be obliged to execute the will of the deceased or only insofar as it leaves their forced estate intact.

E.g    Hector, a widower, has two children, Gilles and Giliane. Giliane has always been the apple of his eye and Gilles must have done something to displease his father, but everyone has forgotten what that was. Anyway, Hector drew up a will leaving his entire estate worth €300,000 to Giliane.

The will is not invalid, but the bequest to Giliane will be reduced to €200,000. Gilles must receive at least one third. Giliane is entitled to her share in the forced portion and the entire disposable portion.

If there are more than one bequest that encroach on the disposable part, then all these bequests will be reduced proportionally.

### Lifetime donations may be clawed back

When all bequests are cancelled, and the heirs do not get the forced estate, some donations made by the deceased in his lifetime may be "clawed back". This begins with the latest donation going back, one donation at a time, until there is a donation that impinges partially on the forced estate. That donation will be reduced, but earlier donations will be left in place.

The beneficiaries of these donations must give back what they have received. If necessary, the heirs will have to ask the court to annul these donations.

If the beneficiary of a lifetime gift is also one of the heirs, he does not have to return the objects or the cash he received. The gift from the deceased may be off-set against what he will inherit. The assumption will be that the donor just wanted to give the beneficiary an advance on his inheritance. In that case, the value of the gift will be taken into account to determine if he has received more than his equal share.

The donor may, however, have wanted to give his heir a bit more than the other heirs. That must be clear from the donation; it should say that the donation is made *bij vooruitmaking en buiten erfdeel / par préciput et hors part,* that is in advance over and above his equal share with the other heirs. The value of the donation is to be taken into account to determine whether an heir has not received more than his fair share (that is his share of the forced share plus the disposable part).

> *If Hector had given everything to Giliane before his death, Gilles can ask the court to reduce that donation so that he receives his half.*

> *However, if Hector makes sure to mention that the donation was "par préciput et hors part", Gilles can only get a third.*

## Insurance policies

Life insurance falls outside the inheritance rules. However, it would be too easy to use life insurance to get around the forced heirship rules. If a life insurance policy is a donation in disguise, it may be added to the estate just as if it were a donation.

If the beneficiary of the policy is also one of the heirs, it is assumed that the policyholder has released the beneficiary of the obligation to return the insurance capital. If he wanted the beneficiary to return the capital, he must make an express statement to that effect (see p. 167).

# USUFRUCT

Usufruct is the Belgian solution intended to provide for some relatives or friends and to give them financial security for the rest of their life. The law uses it as a solution in the following situations:

If the deceased has children, the surviving spouse inherits the usufruct of his estate. They are taken care of for the rest of their lives; they can live in the family home and use the furniture, collect the interest from the bank accounts and bonds, and the dividends from his investments. Nevertheless, in his will the deceased may have limited the usufruct. However, he must take account of the forced heirship rules.

When there are no children, the surviving spouse inherits the community property in full, but only usufruct of the separate property of the deceased. That will return to the family of the deceased when the surviving spouse dies. However, it is possible to deny the family that by drawing up a will without any restriction under the forced heirship rules.

The registered partner also receives the usufruct, but only on the family home and furniture. That would not include the savings of the deceased. However, the deceased could give the partner the usufruct over his savings by drawing up a will. That being said, in your will you could also deny the registered partner the usufruct of the family home and furniture, because he or she is not a forced heir.

When you draw up your will, you can draw inspiration from these solutions if you want to give someone financial security for the rest of their live or for a period of time.

## WHAT IS USUFRUCT?

The word "usufruct" comes from the Latin "usus" (the use) and "fructus" (the fruit). It is the right to use an object and to receive the income. In legalese it is a "right in rem", not just a contract like a lease that can be terminated by the other party.

The spouse who has the usufruct, can use the car and the furniture, live in the house without paying rent, let it out and collect the rent as he likes. However, he cannot sell the property without the agreement of the owners.

The children are the owners, but on paper only. This is called "bare ownership" (*blote eigendom / nue propriété*). The bare owner cannot sell the assets without the agreement of the surviving spouse either.

## Usufruct in practice

For a house, usufruct is the right to use the house. As an "usufructier", you can live in it, but you can also let it out and receive the rent, while you live in smaller accommodation. If you have the usufruct, you do not only have the enjoyment and the use of the property, you also have to pay for all the expenses related to the property (the annual real estate tax, maintenance and repairs, refurbishment, etc ... ). The cost of major repairs to the main structure of the building (walls, roof, etc... ) is for the bare owners

For shares and bonds, usufruct is the right to collect and use the dividends or interest therein. The shares or bonds are usually put in one bank account in the name of the bare owners (the children) with the dividends and interest being paid into an account in the name of the surviving parent. An important issue is who can exercise the voting right in the company; the company's articles of association usually determine that. It is the person with the voting right who determines who will run the company and decide whether and when dividends are paid out.

If you have the usufruct on a savings account, you can collect the interest paid on the account, but you cannot do anything with the capital.

Where the deceased has invested his savings in capitalisation products, such as Sicavs, where the income is automatically added to the capital, the usufruct of the surviving spouse does not give them much. They will have to come to some agreement with the heirs and conversion of usufruct is probably the only solution.

## The drawbacks of usufruct

The inconvenience of usufruct is that it does not give you the right to sell the house, or the investments without the agreement of the bare owners, i.e. the children or the family.

if the children are under 18, you will need the authorisation of the justice of the peace. In general, he will be reluctant to authorise a sale that could result in the children losing their inheritance, unless there is a real need, e.g. because you are moving abroad and need to purchase property there.

Generally, when there is a good understanding with the children, usufruct does not pose a problem. They generally accept that the family assets belong to both their parents. In addition, the surviving parent still owns half of the family assets, and she can spend them, all they will have left is what will have come from their father's inheritance.

If you fear your children will create problems, you can take some preventive action. For example, the parents can deny the children the right to ask for conversion of usufruct.

The situation is more awkward when the children inherit the bare ownership while the usufruct is given to their mother's new spouse or registered partner. The position of the stepfather or partner can be strengthened, e.g. by giving him the maximum disposable part on top of the usufruct, or by changing your marriage contract, etc ...

If there is a portfolio of bonds and shares in the estate, one question is who can manage that portfolio and who can decide to sell and reinvest. The surviving spouse will prefer bonds with a high return or Sicavs (unit trusts) that pay out a dividend, while the bare owners will prefer to maintain the capital or capitalisation Sicavs. They will have to find some agreement and here conversion is usually the solution as well.

## USUFRUCT DOES NOT HAVE TO BE FOR LIFE

In principle, usufruct is granted to the surviving spouse for the rest of their life. Upon their death it extinguishes and the bare owners become full owners.

E.g.　When Charles married Katrien, she got on quite well with his sons; they were quite close in age. When Charles died, things turned sour. James and Harry inherited the bare ownership of his estate.

　　　During Katrien's lifetime that is not worth much if they cannot get their hands on dad's estate, but Katrien does not plan to die young.

## Conversion of usufruct

Both the bare owners and the surviving spouse or partner can agree to buy each other out. This is called "conversion". That is, of course, if they are not on speaking terms and cannot agree to sell the property together and split the cash.

If there are several properties and assets, they can decide to divide those up.

The surviving spouse can pay the heirs to have full ownership of the property. Alternatively, she can waive the usufruct, for compensation. The heirs can pay her a sum of money or they can agree to pay a guaranteed annuity for the rest of her life; that annuity should be index linked.

If the surviving spouse inherits the usufruct with the children of the deceased, both the children and the spouse can ask for conversion in court. That can solve some problems.

> *Katrien can take the initiative; she may have to do that since she has to pay inheritance tax. She can ask James and Harry that they sell her their bare ownership or buy her usufruct.*

> *James and Harry can also ask Katrien to sell them the usufruct or to pay them to get the full ownership of the property.*

The good thing is that the family home is protected.

> *Katrien cannot be obliged to sell it or to buy the children out. She is always sure she can live there. And when it becomes too big, she can look for a tenant and spend the rent on something smaller.*

However, if the surviving spouse inherits with heirs other than the children of the deceased, e.g. his brothers and sisters, only the surviving spouse can ask for conversion.

Nieces and nephews can never oblige the surviving spouse or partner to sell them the usufruct or buy them out.

## The value of usufruct

How do you put a value on usufruct or on the bare ownership? Since the usufruct is linked to the life expectancy of the surviving spouse, the value of the usufruct is calculated by taking account of the age and life expectancy of the surviving spouse and an interest rate. That is an actuarial calculation. These actuarial figures are not the same as the figures used to calculate the inheritance tax.

> *if Katrien is 62 when Charles dies, the usufruct she has is worth 57% of his estate.*

This is where the young stepmother rule kicks in. The value of Katrien's usufruct must be calculated as if she was 20 years older than Charles' oldest child.

> *If his oldest is 56, Katrien's usufruct is calculated as if she was 76. The value of the usufruct for a 76 year old is much less than for a 62 year old; that would be about 40%. That does not give her much.*

## Deny your heirs the right of conversion

You can deny your heirs the right to ask for the termination of the usufruct. This can be useful to protect the surviving spouse if you expect that your heirs will want to cash in on your inheritance.

However, the right to ask for conversion cannot be denied to the children from a previous relation when they inherit with the surviving spouse.

> *Because Katrien is their stepmother, Charles cannot deny his sons the right to ask for conversion of the usufruct. They can always ask the court to oblige Katrien to buy them out or let them buy her out.*

Moreover, you cannot deny your spouse the right to buy out the children as the bare owners of the family home and he/she can always refuse to be bought out in respect of the family home.

# COMMUNITY PROPERTY

Marriage is an institution that has effects of a personal nature between husband and wife (you promise each other fidelity and you agree to support each other) and between them and their children. Marriage also has economic and financial implications: you must support each other and the children financially; you cannot sell the family home (even if you own it) or terminate the rental agreement for the family home.

There are also rules that deal with matrimonial property; your matrimonial property regime determines which set of rules apply. The most important distinction is whether you have community property and if so, whether everything is, or is not, in community property?

## WHICH MARRIAGE CONTRACT?

When a couple buys property the notary will ask them what marriage contract they have. You may well wonder what business of his that is; isn't that a private matter?

This is where cultures clash. Prenuptial agreements deal with the effects of divorce; marriage contracts deal with ownership of assets and liability for each other's debts.

### Prenuptial agreements

In Anglo Saxon countries, a prenuptial agreement is a contract signed before marriage or a civil union to deal with the possibility of divorce or a breakup of the marriage. The content can vary, but commonly they include provisions relating to the division of property, spousal support, the terms for the forfeiture of assets in case of a divorce on the grounds of adultery, guardianship over the children, etc.

These are countries that, as a rule, do not have community property; each spouse has his own assets. The wife may not have been working and not own anything. That can create problems when the marriage ends in divorce or upon death. That is why the divorce court may make a property adjustment order or a pension sharing order.

Generally speaking what the court does is to ascertain the assets and divide these by two. That is an oversimplification; the court may give the spouse less if the couple did not have a long marriage, if one spouse has inherited the bulk of the family assets, or if the couple had signed a prenuptial agreement.

## Marriage contracts

Unlike prenuptial agreements, marriage contracts are entered into for a number of reasons, not merely to cater for divorce. They only provide for the ownership and the liability of the family's assets; they do not dictate in advance the financial settlement upon a divorce.

Marriage contracts are not just a private contract. They are entered into before an independent notary and they are legally binding on third parties, including Belgian courts and creditors who try to collect debts.

When a notary asks you what marriage contract you have, what he really wants to know is what your matrimonial property regime is. The matrimonial regime may provide that husband and wife will have a marital estate (community property), and it may determine what properties are included in that marital estate, how and by whom it is managed, and how it will be divided and inherited at the end of the marriage.

In civil law countries, even if a couple has not signed a marriage contract before they married, they have a default matrimonial property regime in law, or, if you prefer, a default marriage contract. Usually that is community property.

In common law countries, the default matrimonial regime is separation of property. Some U.S. States are an exception; they are known as community property States: Arizona, California, Idaho, Louisiana, Nevada, New Mexico, Texas, Washington, and Wisconsin.

### The default marriage contract in Belgium

The default marriage contract for Belgians marrying in Belgium is a mix between community property and separate property. Everything spouses acquire during their marriage is community property. Everything they owned before they married, receive or inherit during the marriage is separate property.

Most people start with nothing; they only have community property. Anything they acquire during their marriage will be deemed to be community property: net earnings, income from personal savings and investments and the house they buy together with a mortgage loan they pay off with their earnings, etc... All bank accounts, whether opened by the husband, by the wife, or on behalf of both spouses, will be deemed to be community property.

Some start with a little advantage in life or inherit during the marriage.

Separate property is the exception. What a spouse owned before they married or what they receive through a donation, a bequest or an inheritance (from relatives or from friends) remains their own. Moreover, when they sell separate property, they can reinvest it and keep it as separate property.

However, it is a question of keeping account of what is separate property. What cannot be proven to be separate property, will be deemed to be community property.

A couple is not obliged to have the default regime. The law proposes two alternatives: full community property or full separation of assets with no community property at all. These are not the only alternatives, and there are many variations of marriage contracts (see p. 153).

Why would one want to change the default marriage contract?

### Full community property

Opting for full community property may be a way of leaving more to one's spouse. A marriage contract that states that all the family assets are community property and that the surviving spouse will receive all the community property can be a valid way of disinheriting the children upon the death of the first parent (see p. 156).

If there are no children, a marriage contract with full community property can be a way of ensuring that the surviving spouse receives all the family assets, and that they do not go to back to the family of the deceased.

### Separation of properties

On the other hand, there are many reasons why one would opt for a full separation of properties with no community property.

The main reason is to protect the estate and the income of the other spouse against one's creditors and to protect some property during the marriage, for instance in case of a bankruptcy. Most debts are debts of the community property, even business debts and tax liabilities. However, if there is no community property, creditors cannot claim money from the spouse.

Another reason is to protect one's estate in case of divorce.

When a married couple divorces, each spouse keeps his own separate property and they split the community property. If a couple does not have community property, each spouse keeps his own belongings. That is bad news for a stay at home husband or wife who did not have any earnings; they are left with nothing. In Belgium, they cannot ask the court for a property adjustment or pension sharing order. The court does not redistribute the family assets. It can, however, order maintenance to allow the beneficiary to keep the standing of living to which they are accustomed.

A final reason for keeping the properties separate is to keep assets in the family. If you have no community property and your wife has been working while you were the stay at home dad, you own nothing. The children inherit their mother's estate and you get the *usufruct* of her assets for the rest of your life.

If you have no children, the surviving spouse gets all of the community property and only the usufruct of the personal estate of your spouse. If there is no community property, you only have the right to use the family assets for the rest of your life. However, it is owned by the family of your spouse. When you die, her brother and sisters, nieces and nephews will get it all. There will be nothing for you to leave to your own nieces and nephews.

## CHANGE YOUR MARRIAGE CONTRACT?

Until a couple of years ago, the procedure for changing a marriage contract required a review by a justice of the peace. When things were urgent, that could take too long. Since 2008, the procedure has been simplified a lot. All that is required is a notarial deed signed by the two spouses.

An inventory listing all the belongings of the spouses and their liabilities and debts is useful, but not required. It is, however, needed if the marriage contract entails a conversion from community property to separate properties or vice versa, but not when it is just a question of changing the modalities. Of course, either spouse can ask that an inventory be drawn up.

When spouses change their marriage contract, a short abstract must be registered with the town hall of the place where they were married. Moreover, the fact that the marriage contract was modified must be published in the Belgian Official Journal. And if one spouse is a self-employed businessman, the change of marriage contract must be registered with the commercial court.

Changing a marriage contract can be relatively quick. It only requires a trip to the notary. What takes time is the transfer of real property; the notary must check the rights of the owner and that can take two to three months. If no real property is involved, things can go much faster. Between husband and wife, the change of marriage contract is immediate. However, vis-à-vis third parties, the new marriage contract only takes effect from the day the abstract is published in the Belgian Official Journal. This takes another ten days at least.

# MARRIAGE CONTRACTS INTERNATIONALLY

These rules apply to a Belgian couple. International situations are more complex, where a Belgian marries a non-Belgian, when two non-Belgians marry in Belgium or when a non-Belgian married couple comes to live in Belgium.

Do they have community property or not?

That is important for the judge who must determine what each spouse takes out of the divorce or what one spouse inherits from the other, for the creditors who have a claim against one spouse or for the tax authorities if they have to collect the tax due by a spouse.

## The international perspective

Under Belgian law, the court can apply the law of the country that the spouses have chosen in their marriage contract for their matrimonial property regime. However, Belgian law does not permit spouses to choose any law other than the law of the country of residence or nationality of either spouse, or the law of the country of their first residence as a married couple.

However, most couples do not choose a law. In that case, Belgian law has some rules to determine what law they would have chosen. We must make a distinction between the situation before and after October 2004. That is because in 2004, the rules were codified. Before that date the principles, the private international law rules, were to be found in the case law.

### You married before 1 October 2004

For couples married before 1 October 2004, Belgium will assume that a couple with the same nationality have adopted the matrimonial property regime of their country.

> *Two British nationals married at the latest on 30 September 2004 are deemed to have full separation of properties, while a French couple would have a system of community property that is very close to that of a Belgian couple.*

For a couple with two different nationalities, Belgium looks at the law of the country where they lived together as a married couple just after their marriage.

### You married on or after 1 October 2004

For a couple married since the Private International Law Code entered into force on 1 October 2004, any couple that had their first habitual residence in Belgium as a married couple (or in any country that has a similar legal system) are deemed to have community property, even if they have the same nationality, with the exception of what they owned before their marriage or what they inherited.

E.g.  *Two British nationals who met in Belgium and married in 2006 will have community property like Belgians if they set up their marital residence in Belgium.*

> *A Belgian who married an Irish national in 2007 and lived in the U.K. first will not have community property. They own everything separately.*

If they did not take up their habitual residence in the same country and they have the same nationality, a couple's national law will be the law of their matrimonial property regime. If they do have not the same nationality, Belgium will assume that they adopted the matrimonial property regime of the law of the country where they were married. The website www.coupleseurope.eu gives a summary of the statutory matrimonial property regimes in the EU Member States, the consequences of divorce and death, the situation of multinational couples and registered and non-registered partners.

## Can anyone sign a marriage contract?

Non Belgians can sign a marriage contract in Belgium, and choose the law that will apply to their matrimonial property regime.

Moreover, they can sign a marriage contract to change the rules that would apply between them under Belgian law. They can opt for community property or change from community property to separate properties. That new matrimonial property regime will then apply to their assets in Belgium and abroad.

They can even agree to convert overseas assets into community property.

Between them ownership is transferred by signing the marriage contract. However, this may not be sufficient to formalise the transfer in the country where the assets are located. It may be necessary, in particular for real property, to register the marriage contract or to pass before a notary in the country where the assets are situated.

However, a couple in this situation would be well advised to make sure that this solution is not contrary to the law of the country where the assets are located.

Furthermore, when the couple leaves Belgium and takes up domicile in another country, that country may not accept the matrimonial property regime agreed in Belgium.

# INHERITANCE TAX

Inheritance tax (*successierechten/droits de succession*) is paid by your heirs on the net value of what they inherit from your estate.

Inheritance tax is only due in Belgium if you were resident in Belgium at the time of your death. If you have left Belgium a few months before your death, Belgian inheritance tax will not be due except on your real property located in Belgium.

The country where the person dies is irrelevant, just like his nationality or the residence of the heir. It is not because someone dies while on holiday in Mexico that Mexican law will apply. If a Belgian resident inherits from a French national living in Switzerland, inheritance tax will not be due in Belgium, except on the real property the deceased has in Belgium.

However, if the deceased was not resident in Belgium, Belgian inheritance tax is due but only on his Belgian real property.

Assuming you are domiciled in Belgium, it must be established whether you have your domicile in:

## Brussels, Flanders or Wallonia?

Belgium is a federal state, divided into three regions that can levy certain taxes, in particular inheritance tax and gift tax. Since 1989, the regions (Brussels Capital, Flanders and Wallonia) acquired the power to change the rates, the taxable basis and introduce exemptions of inheritance tax and gift tax. It was not until 1996 that they used these powers.

Flanders introduced a reduced rate for family-owned businesses and a very low gift tax rate for donations of movables. The other regions have followed suit. All the regions have changed their inheritance and gift tax rates, for a while Wallonia had a top rate of 90%.

We now have three inheritance tax codes. Fortunately, the core of the law is the same, so that we can still summarise the law while pointing out a few differences relating to tax rates and personal allowances and exemptions.

Please note that it is only the inheritance tax that has become a regional tax, the inheritance law and the rules on succession, as well as the rules on conflict of laws are the same for the whole of Belgium.

Whether your heirs will pay Brussels, Flemish or Walloon inheritance tax depends on the region where you were living. All inheritance tax will be due in the region where you were living, even if you own property in another region. However, if you have moved from one region to another in the last five years before your death, it is the region where you had your residence for the longest period of time that is determinant.

### In which region do you live?

If you live in Ostend or Liège, it is rather obvious in which region you live and what inheritance tax rules apply. Confusing is that in some Flemish towns, the official language is Dutch (or Flemish), but that French may be used for certain administrative purposes, and vice versa. These are the so-called "municipalities with language facilities" around the Brussels Region and on the language border.

The Brussels Capital Region includes the 19 municipalities of Anderlecht, Oudergem/Auderghem, Sint-Agatha-Berchem/Berchem-Sainte-Agathe, Brussels, Etterbeek, Evere, Vorst/Forest, Ganshoren, Elsene/Ixelles, Jette, Koekelberg, Sint-Jans-Molenbeek/Molenbeek-Saint-Jean,Sint-Gillis Saint-Gilles, Sint-Joost-ten-Node/Saint-Josse-ten-Noode, Schaarbeek/ Schaerbeek, Ukkel/Uccle, Watermaal-Bosvoorde/Watermael-Boitsfort, Sint-Lambrechts-Woluwe / Woluwe-Saint-Lambert, Sint-Pieters-Woluwe/ Woluwe- Saint-Pierre.

The Flemish Region (het Vlaams Gewest) includes the Flemish provinces of West and Oost Vlaanderen, Antwerpen, Limburg and Vlaams Brabant. The municipalities of Drogenbos, Kraainem, Linkebeek, Sint-Genesius-Rode, Wemmel and Wezembeek-Oppem, around Brussels are in the Flemish Region, as are the Flemish language borders towns of Mesen, Ronse, Spiere-Helkijn, Bever, Herstappe and Voeren.

The Walloon Region (la Région wallonne) consists of the provinces of Hainaut, Liège, Luxembourg, Namur and Brabant wallon. The language border towns of Comines-Warneton, Enghien, Flobecq and Mouscron are part of the Walloon region, as are all the towns in the German language area.

# HOW MUCH INHERITANCE TAX?

Inheritance tax is payable by each heir on his share of the net value of the estate of the deceased.

In the inheritance tax return, the heirs will have to list all the assets in the estate, as well as some assets that are not in the estate anymore, put a value on those, deduct certain debts and liabilities and explain how much each of them gets.

## First, add up all the assets in the estate

To start with, all the assets owned by the deceased at the time of his death are liable to inheritance tax. That is his share in the community property he has with his spouse (normally that is one half), and his own separate property. What the deceased owns is determined according to the rules of civil law. E.g. an usufruct that the deceased had extinguishes upon his death, it must not be reported in the inheritance tax return.

The tax is calculated on the net value of the property distributed to each heir. That is the gross value less the liabilities and debts the deceased had at the time of his death.

Inheritance tax is payable by the heirs on the share they inherit in the inheritance, assuming that they have accepted the inheritance.

In principle, all the heirs get an equal share but if an heir receives more in the will, he will pay more tax.

## And then add some more

There are some rules that adjust the value of the estate. These have been introduced to counter certain forms of inheritance tax planning.

### I.O.U.s

If the deceased has stated in his will that he owes an amount of money, that will be considered to be a bequest. It would be too easy to remember in your will that you owe money to a friend. The debt cannot be deducted from the value of the estate and inheritance tax will be due.

Likewise any other I.O.U. may be deemed to be a gift in disguise; inheritance tax will be due unless gift tax has been paid on the amount of the debt. Even then, a debt acknowledged in favour of the deceased's direct heirs is never deductible, even if gift tax has been paid.

### Gifts that take effect upon the death of the donor

Any donation of movables that is made subject to the condition precedent of the death of the donor is liable to inheritance tax.

### Gifts in the marriage contract

If a couple has community property, each of them owns half of the community property. When one spouse dies, the other will get his half, the part of the deceased is added to his estate. Sometimes the marriage contract states that the surviving spouse will receive more than half of the community property (see p. 156), in that case any euro over the value of half the estate will be liable to inheritance tax.

### Gifts in the last three years

Anything given away by the deceased in the last three years of his life is added to the value of his estate and will be subject to inheritance tax, unless gift tax has been paid.

Even if gift tax has been paid, then the donation is added to the value of the estate but merely to determine the inheritance tax rate.

However, if no gift tax has been paid, the donation will be added to the estate and subject to inheritance tax. In that case, the only way to avoid inheritance tax completely is for the donor to outlive the donation by more than three years. That is why a hand to hand donation or a donation from one bank account to another are popular estate planning techniques, as long as the donor lives for another three years after the donation.

If the tax authorities can prove that the deceased owned certain tangible movable assets in the last three years of his life, they can add these assets to the estate and claim inheritance tax from the heirs even if they have not actually received the goods.

If the heirs or legatees, or the tax authorities, can prove who has received the assets, that beneficiary will have to pay inheritance tax. However, if the beneficiary is not an heir nor a legatee, the heirs or legatees are liable to pay the inheritance tax, but they can recover the tax from the real beneficiaries.

## Contracts to the benefit of a third party (life insurance)

This rule is a little wider than just life insurance policies, but life insurance is the classic example. It covers any contract between the deceased and someone else (e.g. the insurance company) to give money, annuities or other valuables to a third party (the beneficiary) when the deceased dies.

Life insurance can also be taken out by an employer on the life of an employee (e.g. in a pension scheme) for his children may be liable to inheritance tax.

However, if the policy was subscribed by the deceased himself, it is not limited to benefits paid at the time of his own death. It also applies to benefits to be paid in the three years before his death or at any time after his death. This offers various possibilities for estate planning (see p. 166).

No inheritance tax is due if gift tax has been paid on the policy.

Also exempt are payments of a capital or an annuity when there is a legal obligation (e.g. a state pension paid to the surviving spouse), or when the policyholder did not have the intention of granting the beneficiary any benefit. The usual example is that of an employee who died on a trip paid for by his employer with an American Express card that happened to have life insurance in favour of the traveller.

The most important exception is group insurance funded by the deceased's employer. There is no inheritance tax on the death benefit paid out under the terms of an obligatory group insurance policy financed by the employer's contributions. However, that is only if the beneficiary is his surviving spouse or his children as long as they are under 21.

Inheritance tax is due, nevertheless, on the part of the insured capital for which the employee had paid voluntary contributions on top of any obligatory contributions. There is no exemption for group insurance taken out by self-employed freelancers or company directors who have self-employed status.

Please note that it is not because inheritance tax is not due that the pension plan will be exempt from income tax; the insurance company will withhold tax at source.

### Usufruct constructions

Because usufruct comes to an end when the person holding the usufruct dies, inheritance tax is not due. However, one could consider buying property with a child (for the bare ownership) and the parent for the usufruct) so that the child has full ownership when the parent dies.

If the taxman can assume that this is a disguised donation to reduce the inheritance tax, he can charge inheritance tax on the full value of the property. The beneficiary must then prove that this was not a disguised gift.

## What value do you give to these assets?

The taxable value of the asset is the sales value at the time of death.

For real property, a notary can help establish the value; the federation of notaries keeps records of the sales prices of properties in Belgium. For real estate outside Belgium, one must in the first place look at the value shown in official documents or deeds. If these are not available, the value is twenty times the annual income for buildings and thirty times for land. If inheritance tax is due in that country, then the value reported for inheritance tax will be the minimum.

For stock in listed companies, we look at the prices which the taxman publishes every month in the Belgian Official Journal (*prijs courant / prix courant*). These prices are the average of the prices in the preceding month. The heirs have the choice between the listing in the first, second or third month following the death.

For the capital and interest of receivables, the value is the nominal value. For perpetual bonds, we take twenty times the annual interest or return. Nevertheless, the heirs can prove that the real value is much less e.g. if the debtor is insolvent (think of bank accounts with Kaupthing Bank).

The value of usufruct is a percentage of the sales value of the assets on which the usufruct is created; the percentage in the table below depends on the age of the beneficiary of the usufruct. If usufruct is given to more than one person, we look at the age of the youngest.

The value of bare ownership is the value of full ownership less the value of usufruct.

To determine the value of an annuity given for the life of a person (the beneficiary or someone else), we multiply the interest with the coefficient in the table below, depending on the age of that person.

| Age of the beneficiary | Coefficient | Percentage |
|:---:|:---:|:---:|
| 0 – 20 | 18 | 72% |
| 21 – 30 | 17 | 68% |
| 31 – 40 | 16 | 64% |
| 41 – 50 | 14 | 56% |
| 51 – 55 | 13 | 52% |
| 56 – 60 | 11 | 44% |
| 61 – 65 | 9.5 | 38% |
| 66 – 70 | 8 | 32% |
| 71 – 75 | 6 | 24% |
| 76 – 80 | 4 | 16% |
| over 81 | 2 | 8% |

Annuities or usufruct granted for a period of time are valued by capitalizing the annual interest or return at 4%; the maximum value is the value for a lifetime annuity or usufruct.

## Deduct debts and liabilities

The tax is calculated on the net value of the property distributed to each heir (assuming they accept the inheritance tax).

That is the gross value less the liabilities and debts the deceased had at the time of his death. In principle, all debts are deductible, including the last hospital bills, and the costs of the funeral.

Debt acknowledged in a will or in favour of the deceased's direct heirs is never deductible even if gift tax has been paid.

# INHERITANCE TAX RATES

Inheritance tax rates vary from one region to another. The applicable rates are those of the region where the deceased lived at the time of his death. Where the beneficiaries live, or where the property is located is irrelevant.

However, if the deceased lived in more than one region in the last five years before his death, we must look at the region where he lived for the longest period of time in the last five years before his death.

## Zero rates and reduced rates

Legacies in favour of the Region where the deceased had his fiscal residence are zero rated.

Flanders exempts shares in certain companies that invest in service flats for elderly people, as well as for forests and certain types of land that are of ecological interest from tax. Wallonia also favours certain types of land with an ecological interest.

Charities benefit from a lower rate in all three regions. The tax rate depends on the region where the deceased had his last tax residence.

There is an exemption from inheritance tax for the transfer of family-owned businesses in the Walloon region, while the Brussels and Flemish regions have a flat rate of 3%. The conditions vary from one region to the other but that is a discussion that falls outside the scope of this book.

## Brussels Capital Region

The inheritance tax is calculated, for each heir separately, on the share they inherit.

The lowest rates are for heirs in the **direct line** (that is between parents and grandparents and the children and grandchildren), and between **spouses** and **registered partners.** Non registered partners pay the highest inheritance tax rates.

Each of these heirs is entitled to a deduction of the first €15,000; that "*abatement*" is tax exempt. Additional – relatively limited – reductions of inheritance tax are granted for children under 21 and for spouses.

| On the band between | | Rate | Tax on previous bands |
|---|---|---|---|
| €0 - €50 000 | | 3% | |
| €50 000 - €100 000 | | 8% | + €1 500 |
| €100 000 - €175 000 | | 9% | + €5 500 |
| €175 0000 - €250 000 | | 18% | + €12 250 |
| €250 000 - €500 000 | | 24% | + €25 750 |
| over €500 000 | | 30% | + €85 750 |

The rates are progressive, that means that the first €50,000 is taxed at 3%. The following €50,000 is taxed at 8%, etc.

*E.g.* *If the share of one heir is €120,000, we can deduct the abatement of €15 000; that leaves €105,000. €105,000 falls in the 100,000 - 175,000 bracket. 105,000 - 100,000 = 5,000 x 9% = 450 + 5,500 = €5,950 tax*

If you own or co-own your **main residence** (and have lived there for five years, except for *force majeure, e.g.* when you have to live in a home), there are reduced rates on that property. These reduced rates just reduce the inheritance tax on the property; any other belongings are taxed at the higher rates.

| On the band between | | Rate | Tax on previous bands |
|---|---|---|---|
| €0 - €50 000 | | 2% | |
| €50 000 - €100 000 | | 5.3% | + €1 000 |
| €100 000 - €175 000 | | 6% | + €3 650 |
| €175 0000 - €250 000 | | 12% | + €8 150 |

Between **brothers and sisters**, the rates are as follows, the tax is still calculated on the share **each of them receives.**

| | | Rate | |
|---|---|---|---|
| €0 - €12 500 | | 20% | |
| €12 500 - €25 000 | | 25% | + €2 500 |
| €25 000 - €50 000 | | 30% | + €5 625 |
| €50 000 - €100 000 | | 40% | + €13 125 |
| €100 000 - €175 000 | | 55% | + €33 125 |
| €175 000 - €250 000 | | 60% | + €74 375 |
| Over €250 000 | | 65% | + €119 375 |

When **nephews and nieces** inherit from their uncles and aunts (and vice versa), the tax runs rise quickly. That is not only because the tax rates are higher, but also because the tax is calculated on the total value of all assets inherited by the nieces and nephews (or uncles and aunts). Everything is added up and the tax is **calculated on the total**.

| €0 | - | €50 000 | 35% | |
|---|---|---|---|---|
| €50 000 | - | €100 000 | 50% | + €17 500 |
| €100 000 | - | €175 000 | 60% | + €42 500 |
| over €175 000 | | | 70% | + €87 500 |

*E.g.* *If you leave €500,000 to ten nieces and nephews, they each receive €50,000, but they do not pay 35%. The tax is 70% on the €325,000 over €175,000, i.e. €227,500 plus €87,500 = €315,000. The tax rate is 63%!*

The rule is the same when **anyone else** inherits (cousins, first cousins once removed, second cousins, non-registered partners, friends, etc). The tax rate is a group rate:

| €0 | - | €50 000 | 40% | |
|---|---|---|---|---|
| €50 000 | - | €75 000 | 55% | + €20 000 |
| €75 000 | - | €175 000 | 65% | + €33 750 |
| over €175 000 | | | 80% | + €98 750 |

*E.g.* *If you leave €400,000 to your partner and €50,000 to two friends, the tax is 80% on the €325,000 over €175,000, i.e. €260,000 plus €98,750 = €358,750. The tax rate is 71.75%!*

There are special rates for legacies to **charities**: 25% for non-profit associations, international associations and foundations, but 12.5% if they are recognised as charitable institutions.

## Flanders

Inheritance tax is calculated, for each heir separately, on the share they inherit.

The lowest rates are for heirs in the **direct line** (that is between parents and grandparents and the children and grandchildren), and between **spouses** and **registered** partners.

Non registered partners or even people living in the same household may be entitled to the same rates.

| On the band between | Rate | Tax on previous bands |
|---|---|---|
| €0 - €50 000 | 3% | |
| €50 000 - €250 000 | 9% | + €1 500 |
| Over €250 000 | 27% | + €19 500 |

Note that the inheritance tax due is calculated **separately** for real estate and moveable assets. Liabilities are set off against the moveable estate, unless they have been specifically incurred to acquire real estate.

The rates are progressive, meaning that the first €50,000 is taxed at 3%. The following €200,000 is taxed at 9%, etc.

E.g.    *If a parent leaves a house worth €400,000 and savings worth €400,000 to his four children, each pays tax on a value of €200,000, the tax is calculated separately for the house and for the savings. Each heir receives €100,000 in the house and €100,000 in the savings. The €100,000 in the house is taxed at 9% on the €50,000 over €50,000 plus €1,500. That is €6,000 in total. The inheritance tax on the savings is calculated in the same way. Each heirs pays €12,000 inheritance tax.*

The surviving spouse or (live-in) partner does not pay inheritance tax on the **family home** or on the usufruct of the family home.

Between **brothers and sisters,** the rates are as follows. The tax is calculated on the share each of them receives. No distinction is made between real property and moveable assets.

| | | |
|---|---|---|
| €0 - €75 000 | 30% | |
| €75 000 - €125 000 | 55% | + €22 500 |
| Over €125 000 | 65% | + €50 000 |

When **anyone else** inherits (cousins, first cousins once removed, second cousins, non-registered partners, friends, etc), the rates go up very quickly. There are higher rates, but the tax is calculated on the share they **all receive together**.

| | | |
|---|---|---|
| €0 - €75 000 | 45% | |
| €75 000 - €125 000 | 55% | + €33 750 |
| Over €125 000 | 65% | + €61 250 |

*E.g.* *If you leave €500,000 to ten nieces and nephews, they each receive €50,000, but they do not pay 450%. The tax is 65% on the €375,000 over €125,000, i.e.243,750 + 61,250 = €305,000. The average tax rate is 61.60%.*

Legacies to **charities** are taxed at the fixed rates of 8.8% for non-profit associations, international associations and foundations. Foreign associations and foundations qualify for these lower rates if they are similar legal entities that are subject to the law of a Member State of the European Economic Area and that have their registered office, head office or principal establishment within the European Economic Area.

## Wallonia

Inheritance tax is calculated, for each heir separately, on the share they inherit.

The lowest rates are for heirs in the **direct line** (that is between parents and grandparents and the children and grandchildren), and between **spouses** and **registered partners**.

| On the band between | | Rate | Tax on previous bands |
|---|---|---|---|
| €0 - €12 500 | | 3% | |
| €12 500 - €25 000 | | 4% | + €375 |
| €25 000 - €50 000 | | 5% | + €875 |
| €50 000 - €100 000 | | 7% | + €2 125 |
| €100 000 - €150 000 | | 10% | + €5 625 |
| €150 000 - €200 000 | | 14% | + €10 625 |
| €200 000 - €250 000 | | 18% | + €17 625 |
| €250 000 - €500 000 | | 24% | + €26 625 |
| over €500 000 | | 30% | + €86 625 |

*E.g.* *If the share of one heir is €120,000, deduct €12,500, and then see in what bracket the balance is (107,500). That is the 100,000 - 150,000 bracket. Deduct the lower number of the bracket from €107,500. That leaves €7,500; take 10% (i.e. €750) and add the tax on the previous bands, €5,625. The total tax is €750 + €5,625 = €6,375.*

Each of these heirs is entitled to a deduction of the first €12,500; that "*abattement*" is tax exempt. There are additional – relatively limited – reductions of inheritance tax for children under 21 and for spouses.

The rates are progressive, that means that the first €12,500 is taxed at 3%. The following €12,500 is taxed at 4%, etc.

If you own or co-own your **main residence** (and have lived there for five years, except for *force majeure, e.g.* when you have to live in a home), there are reduced rates on that property. These reduced rates just reduce the inheritance tax on the property; any other belongings are taxed at the higher rates.

| On the band between | | | Rate | Tax on previous bands |
|---|---|---|---|---|
| €0 | - | €25 000 | 1% | |
| €25 000 | - | €50 000 | 2% | + €250 |
| €50 000 | - | €175 000 | 5% | + €750 |
| €175 000 | - | €250 000 | 12% | + €7 000 |
| €250 000 | - | €500 000 | 24% | + €16 000 |
| over €500 000 | | | 30% | + €76 000 |

Between **brothers and sisters,** the rates are as follows. The tax is calculated on the share each of them receives.

| €0 | - | €12 500 | 20% | |
|---|---|---|---|---|
| €12 500 | - | €25 000 | 25% | + €2 500 |
| €25 000 | - | €75 000 | 35% | + €5 625 |
| €75 000 | - | €175 000 | 50% | + €23 125 |
| over €175 000 | | | 65% | + €73 125 |

When **nephews and nieces** inherit from their uncles and aunts:

| €0 | - | €12 500 | 25% | |
|---|---|---|---|---|
| €12 500 | - | €25 000 | 30% | + €3 125 |
| €25 000 | - | €75 000 | 40% | + €6 875 |
| €75 000 | - | €175 000 | 55% | + €26 875 |
| over €175 000 | | | 70% | + €81 875 |

When **anyone else** inherits (cousins, first cousins once removed, second cousins, non-registered partners, friends, etc):

| €0 | - | €12 500 | 30% | |
|---|---|---|---|---|
| €12 500 | - | €25 000 | 35% | + €3 750 |
| €25 000 | - | €75 000 | 60% | + €8 125 |
| over €75 000 | | | 80% | + €38 125 |

*E.g.*  *If you leave €400,000 to your partner and €50,000 to two friends, your partner will pay €38,125 on the first €75,000 and 80% on everything over that. That is 80% of €325,000 plus 38,125 = 298,125, or 74.53%.*

*Your friends will pay 60% on €25,000 plus €8,125, in total €23,125 and that is 46.25%.*

Legacies to **charities** are taxed at the fixed rate of 7% for non-profit associations, international associations and foundations. Foreign associations and foundations may qualify for these lower rates if they have a working office within the European Economic Area.

# THE INHERITANCE TAX RETURN

Filing the inheritance tax return is an obligation for the heirs and the general legatees. If the deceased has appointed an executor in his will, the executor may file the inheritance tax return but he cannot be obliged to do so.

You can obtain a standard form from the tax office, but that will not help you much; it is a blank form on which you must list the belongings of the deceased and his debts.

The assistance of a notary or adviser is advisable; it is not easy to determine what is in the deceased's estate. A lot depends on the marriage contract and whether there is community property, some donations must be disregarded, and then one has to look whether there is a will. Finally, there are a few tax rules that are important to know about.

The tax authorities calculate the tax and confirm how much tax is due by each heir.

Each heir or legatee is liable for the inheritance tax on the share he receives in the inheritance. Other beneficiaries have to pay the inheritance tax on what they receive as well, but to make it easier for the taxman, he can claim the inheritance tax due by other beneficiaries from the heirs and general legatees.

The inheritance tax is due two months after the end of the deadline for filing the inheritance tax return (six, seven or eight months afterwards). Interest for late payment is due at the statutory rate of 7 per cent.

The tax must be paid in cash, by bank transfer. However, the heirs can opt to pay the inheritance tax by donating works of art from the estate; there is a special procedure to value the work of art and to determine that the artist is internationally recognised.

# A FEW EXAMPLES

## The O'Donnells in Flanders

Helen and Sean O'Donnell live in Leuven (Flanders). They own a house worth €500,000, and savings of €200,000. Sean also has €100,000 he inherited from his mother. They have three children.

| Estate: | | | Sean | Helen |
|---|---|---|---|---|
| | house in Leuven: | €500,000 | 250,000 | 250,000 |
| | Savings: | €200,000 | 100,000 | 100,000 |
| | Inheritance: | €100,000 | 100,000 | |
| | Total: | €800,000 | 450,000 | 350,000 |

Sean has not drawn up a will. When he dies, Helen is 61, the usufruct she inherits is valued at 38% of Sean's estate, that is 38% of €250,000 for the house and 38% of the other possessions, i.e. €76,000.

No inheritance tax is due on the house between husband and wife.

The inheritance tax on Sean's other possessions (his savings) is 3% on the first €50,000 and 9% on the €26,000 on top of that. In total €3.840.

The children inherit the bare ownership. That is valued at 100 − 38 = 62% of the assets, that is 62% of €250,000 for the house (€155,000, or €51,666 for each of the three children), and 62% of the other possessions (62% of €200,000 = €124,000 or €41,333 per child). In Flanders (and only in Flanders), the tax is calculated separately for the house and the possessions.

Each of the children pays tax on €51,666 for the house (3% of 50,000 = 1,500, plus 9% of 1,666 = 150, it total €1,650). They also pay 3% tax on the €41,333 (the other possessions), that is €1,240).

Each child pays €2,890 inheritance tax.

Upon the first death, the inheritance tax is €12,510. That is 2.78% of the value of Sean's estate.

When Helen passes away, the usufruct ends, and the children become full owners of Sean's estate.

They each inherit a third of Helen's half of the house (1/3 x 250,000 = 83,333 on which the tax is €4,500) and a third of the savings (1/3 x 100,000 = 33,333 on which the inheritance tax is €1,000).

Upon the second death, the total inheritance tax is 3 x (4,500 + 1,000) = 16,500. (4.71%).

# The Berglunds in Brussels

Per and Kristina Berglund live in Ixelles (Brussels). They own a house in Ixelles worth €800,000, with a mortgage of €300.000 and savings of €200,000. Kristina owns a house in Sweden with her brother that they inherited from their parents; it is valued at €500,000. They have three children.

|  |  |  | Per | Kristina |
|---|---|---|---|---|
| Estate: | house Ixelles: | €800,000 | 400,000 | 400,000 |
| | Mortgage: | -€300,000 | -150,000 | -150,000 |
| | Savings: | €200,000 | 100,000 | 100,000 |
| | Inheritance: | €250,000 | - | 250,000 |
| | Total : | €950,000 | 350,000 | 600,000 |

When Kristina dies, she left her share in the house in Sweden to Per. Per is 69 and the usufruct he inherits is valued at 32% of her estate, that is 32% of 250,000 for the house (400,000 – 150,000) and 32% of her share in the savings, that is 32% of €100,000, or €32,000.
The inheritance tax is calculated on the value of Kristina's estate; that is €80,000 + 32,000 + 250,000 = 362,000.

The first €15,000 is exempt. The inheritance tax is 3% on the first €50,000, 8% on the next bracket of €50,000, 9% on the following bracket of 75,000 and 18% on the bracket between 175,000 and 250,000. That means that the tax on the first €250,000 is €25,750. On the bit between 347,000 and 250,000, i.e. 97,000, the tax is 24%. Per will be paying €49,030, but he gets a tax reduction of €2,590 on the family home. The bill will come to 46,440.

The bare ownership that the children inherit is 68% of (€400,000 – 150,000 + 100,000 for the savings), that €238,000 or €79,333 each.

The first €15,000 is exempt. The inheritance tax is 3% on the first bracket of €50,000 and 8% on the remaining €14,333. Each pays €2,646.64 but gets a tax reduction of €1,353.33 on his share in the family home. In total they pays €1,293.31 in inheritance tax each.

In total, the inheritance tax upon the first death is €46,440 + 3 x €1,293.31 = €50,319.93. That is 8.39% of an estate worth €600,000.

When Per dies, the usufruct on Kristina's estate disappears, and the children become full owners of his estate. However, they also inherit Kristina's share in the house in Sweden and pay tax on that again.

They each inherit a third of Per's estate (400,000 – 150,000 + 100,000 + 250,000), that is €600,000 or €200,000 per child. They can deduct €15,000, and on €185,000 they pay €14,050 each. On the family home, they get a credit of €2,766.66

Upon the second death, the total inheritance tax is 3 x (14,050 - 2,766.66) = €11,283.33 x 3 = 33,850.02; that is 5.64%).

Note that no inheritance tax is due in Sweden on the Swedish property, but Belgian inheritance tax is due. Moreover, the property in Sweden is taxed twice in Belgium, first when Per inherits it, and then again when he dies and the children inherit. Some estate planning may be useful.

# CROSS BORDER SUCCESSIONS

A succession can cross borders if a person either has a domicile in two countries, inherits from a person domiciled in another country, inherits or owns real property in another country, or has heirs living in another country.

When there are two, or more, countries involved, there may be a conflict of inheritance rules but there may also be double inheritance tax.

## DOMICILE AND RESIDENCE

Both for the inheritance rules and for the inheritance tax, a distinction must be made as to whether the deceased has his residence in Belgium or not.

If he is resident in Belgium, his entire estate will be inherited in accordance with the Belgian rules (only real property outside Belgium will not be passed on according to local law). Inheritance tax will be due on his entire estate, in Belgium and abroad, and there may be double taxation.

If he is resident outside Belgium, only his real property in Belgium is liable to Belgian inheritance tax and follows the Belgian inheritance rules.

### What is residence?

For most people this is straightforward; it is the address where you live. There is no minimum duration of so many days per year or of so many years before your death. However, there must be a certain degree of permanence or continuity. It is the place you call "home".

Residence is the real criterion but you may be assimilated to having a residence in Belgium if you have the seat of your fortune in Belgium. The "seat of your fortune" is the centre of your family relations or the centre of your business relations and economic interests. That is the place from where your property is administered. It is not necessarily the same as the place where the assets are effectively located.

Whether you have your residence or the seat of your fortune in Belgium is a matter of fact. The tax authorities have the burden of proof. However, a person registered in the civil register of a Belgian municipality is deemed to be a resident until proven otherwise. Furthermore, a person who is married is deemed to be resident in the country where his family is established even if he is not registered with the commune.

> *Jean-François is French and has been sent to work in Belgium for his employer. His family stays in France. He dies during one of his trips to Belgium. He has maintained his domicile in France.*

The taxman will take the simplified view that your residence is the address where you are registered in the commune, the address on your identity card and the address where you receive your income tax return. However, you can disagree and prove that you have your main residence in another country. In that case, you are well advised not to be taxed as a Belgian resident.

> *Jean-Luc is a Belgian who moved to Latvia when he retired. He bought a house there. When he fell ill, he came back regularly for treatment because he feels more comfortable speaking French with his doctors. He dies in Belgium during one of his trips.*

> *That he died in Belgium does not change anything to the fact that he is not an Belgian resident. No Belgian inheritance tax will be due on his estate unless he had kept real property in Belgium.*

## Double residence

There can be a problem if you have two or more residences. You risk paying inheritance tax on your entire estate in both countries. In that case, we need to determine which one is your main residence.

Belgium has two treaties to prevent double inheritance tax, one with France and one with Sweden. The treaty with Sweden is irrelevant because Sweden no longer has inheritance tax. The treaty with France sets a hierarchy of criteria: (1) the permanent home of the deceased meaning the centre of his vital interests, or, in other words, the place with which he had the closest personal links, (2) the place of his principal abode, (3) if he lives in both countries for an equal amount of time, the country of which he is a national and (4) if he is a national of a third country, the tax administrations will have to come to an agreement (after he dies).

If you have a residence in any country other than France, there is no treaty to solve the problem of double residence and you will need to make sure that it is clear which is your main residence.

You can plan your estate by leaving Belgium (see p. 115).

# Residence and domicile

You may have a problem of a different nature if you have a Belgian residence and a U.K. domicile, or a domicile in another common law country. In Belgium, residence is the address where you live, in the U.K. domicile is something that stays with you like British nationality even if you have no address in the U.K.

You can have a domicile of origin (because you were born in the U.K.) or a domicile of choice (because you chose to live there permanently or indefinitely). However, when you come to live in Belgium, you remain domiciled in the U.K. A British couple who comes to live in Belgium for work may still have a U.K. domicile because they have kept a house there, because they may still be a member of a club there, and because they still say they are "going home" when they visit their family.

It is possible to give up your domicile of origin but you must have displayed your intention to leave the U.K. permanently. You will have to make the final choice to take up Belgian domicile and to abandon your U.K. domicile.

# Diplomats

Diplomats and their family do not have Belgian residence. They are considered to have maintained their domicile abroad, unless they have Belgian nationality or unless they were already domiciled in Belgium before being posted to Belgium.

Members of permanent delegations to the Council of NATO and to the EU, as well as certain high officials in international organisations like NATO, the Belgian-Luxembourg Economic Union, the OECD, and the International Cotton Institute have diplomatic status as well.

Members of foreign consulates, and their families, have a similar status provided they do not pursue any commercial activities in Belgium. Honorary consuls are not diplomats.

## Officials of international organisations

Belgium hosts a large number of international organisations and grants their members of staff certain tax benefits. In general, they are not liable to Belgian income tax for the remuneration they receive from their organisation, and sometimes they have an exception of domicile for inheritance tax purposes. That depends on the treaty signed by their organisation with Belgium.

### EU officials

Many officials of the EU Institutions (and their families) who came to Belgium to work for the Institutions are not domiciled in Belgium. In accordance with the Protocol on the Privileges and Immunities of the European Union, they keep their domicile in the EU Member State from where they were recruited.

For most of them that is also the country of their nationality.

E.g.    *An Irishman who came to work for the European Parliament in Brussels in 1997 coming from Ireland has kept his domicile in Ireland; his estate is liable to the Irish inheritance tax, the Capital Acquisition Tax (CAT).*

However, if they were recruited from another country, they have their domicile in that country.

*An Italian recruited to work in the European Council in Brussels while he was living and working in Luxembourg will find that he has kept his domicile in Luxemburg and that his estate is liable to Luxembourg inheritance tax.*

An EU official cannot choose to change domicile when in service. However, if he stays in Belgium upon retirement he will become a Belgian resident, both for the inheritance rules and for the inheritance tax.

The exemption of domicile also applies to the spouses of the deceased, to the extent that they are not separately engaged in an occupation, and to their dependent children as long as they are dependent on and in the care of the EU official.

Nevertheless, because they are really living in Belgium, they would have their residence in Belgium. Even if no inheritance is due on the entire estate, their inheritance would pass to their children in accordance with the Belgian inheritance rules, including the forced heirship rules.

### NATO officials

There are two treaties that deal with the tax situation of people working for NATO. The Agreement between the Parties to the North Atlantic Treaty regarding the Status of their Forces (London, 19 June 1951) and the Agreement on the status of the North Atlantic Treaty Organization, National Representatives and International Staff (Ottawa, 20 September 1951).

During their stay in Belgium, members of a military force or of a civilian component, who are in Belgium only because they are a member of a force or civilian component do not have their residence or domicile in Belgium for the purposes of taxation, except if they are Belgian nationals. They are deemed to have kept their domicile in the country where they were living before coming to live in Belgium.

Under the Ottawa agreement, members of the NATO International Staff who come to work in Belgium do not keep their tax domicile in the state where they were resident at the time of their recruitment. The only exception is for "Representatives" of an EU Member State (including representatives, advisers and technical experts of delegations as reported by the Member State), and for the Executive Secretary of NATO, the Co-ordinator of North Atlantic Defence Production and any other permanent officials of similar rank (to be agreed with the Ministry of Foreign Affairs).

### What does this mean?

The Protocol and international agreements give an exemption of domicile for inheritance tax only, but not for the inheritance rules nor for the gift tax.

Even if an EU official living in Belgium is deemed to be domiciled in his country of origin for inheritance tax, he is effectively domiciled in Belgium for the inheritance rules; this may limit his freedom to make wills and in Belgium he will have to take account of the forced heirship rules (he cannot disinherit his children or his spouse).

However, as long as he works for the European Institutions, he will be considered not to be domiciled in Belgium: Belgian inheritance tax will be due in Belgium if he has property in Belgium.

## Expatriates

Foreign employees can benefit from expatriate tax status for non-Belgian executives or skilled specialists. This tax regime is based on the assumption that the employees have maintained their residence in another country even if they are effectively living in Belgium with their families. The status is granted by the tax administration following an application in which the employee proves he has kept the centre of his personal and economic interests outside Belgium.

The expatriate tax regime does not, however, provide an exemption from inheritance tax.

When an expatriate executive dies while living in Belgium, his estate will be inherited in accordance with the Belgian inheritance rules and his heirs will pay Belgian inheritance tax. However, his heirs may prove that he had not acquired a Belgian domicile because he has a residence in another country that is his main residence and because he had not been here long enough.

# CONFLICTS OF SUCCESSION RULES

Each country has its own rules to determine what constitutes a valid will, who is an heir when the deceased has not made a will, whether the children and the spouse have a reserved portion, how the estate or undivided property is administered and distributed.

## Inheritance rules

That is just one layer of rules. Each country also has private international law rules that determine which jurisdiction will answer these questions. Countries may have different solutions, but they may also use different connecting factors. For a long time, this was nationality. Nowadays, habitual residence is the privileged connecting factor. Common law countries work with domicile and that is wider than residence.

### Domicile vs. residence

If you are a Belgian resident, the Belgian inheritance rules apply to your entire estate, but the law stops at the border. Real property in other countries will be transferred to your heirs in accordance with the local rules.

However, you may have maintained your domicile of origin, and in that case the rules might conflict. It is rarely a public authority or the tax authorities that raise questions, but one group of heirs may find the rules in the other jurisdiction more advantageous while the other group will find more in the Belgian rules.

There is no clear solution to combine both, and sometimes, it is a question of choosing the right jurisdiction, and being the first to do so, as the case of the dead solicitor shows. Mr Davies had executed a will in the U.K. in favour of an uncle and leaving nothing to his mother and siblings. When he died suddenly, his fiancée quickly wrapped up his affairs with probate in the U.K. However, she kept the family in the dark for four months; they even received a text message from the deceased.

The family challenged the administration of the estate, claiming that Mr Davies was domiciled in Belgium when he died and that the will was invalid. However, he was living in Paris with his fiancée, but also stayed in Belgium at his fiancée's home at weekends. If his family had made the case that he was domiciled in Belgium then the will could have been declared null and void, and his family would have inherited in accordance with Belgian law. The High Court upheld Mr Davies' domicile.

Fortunately, most successions are settled on a non-contentious basis. Even then there may be conflicting rules.

### Wills

The laws in other jurisdictions take a wide range of approaches to the validity of wills as to their form and the validity as to their substance. Belgium does not allow joint wills (wills made by two people in one document) or mutual wills. Agreements as to future successions (successions not yet opened) are not allowed.

A handwritten will may be acceptable in common law countries, but it may not have enough information to allow the probate judge to appoint an executor. An international will is only accepted in countries that have introduced the international will. Apart from Belgium, that is Bosnia and Herzegovina, Canada, Cyprus, Ecuador, France, Italy, Libya, Niger, Portugal, Slovenia and Yugoslavia.

### Intestate successions

As to the question who inherits in the absence of a will, the answer is usually the same. Generally, as in Belgium, that is the wife and children, the parents, the grandparents, etc … However, the portions they receive vary from one jurisdiction to another.  The website www.successions-europe.eu can give you the beginning of an answer.

### The forced heirship rules

Most legal systems protect the near relatives of a deceased person who tries to disinherit them. The protection commonly takes the form of a reserved portion of the estate but that mechanism is not recognised in other countries.  In common law countries certain heirs may apply to the court on the ground that the deceased's will does not make reasonable financial provision for the applicant. www.successions-europe.eu can help find the answers.

Common law jurisdictions have difficulties grappling with the idea of a clawback under the forced heirship rules. They would not accept that a forced heir would be able to renege on any donations made by the deceased during his lifetime.

### The administration of the estate

We have already had a chance to explain the different rules for the administration of an estate, including how the estate or undivided property is administered and distributed. That is only part of the difference.

There are also the rules relating to property owned as a joint tenant that passes on the deceased's death to the surviving joint tenant or a revocable trust that may form part of the deceased's estate in some States.

On the continent matrimonial property can be organised so that it passes before the application of the inheritance rules.

# The European Succession Regulation

The European Commission acknowledges that different succession laws in different countries make it difficult to settle international successions within the European Union. To simplify the procedures for settling such international successions and to unify and simplify the inheritance rules for cross-border successions, Regulation N° 650/2012 on jurisdiction, applicable law, recognition and enforcement of decisions and authentic instruments in matters of succession and the creation of a European Certificate of Succession has been adopted.

The Regulation must be implemented by the EU Member States by 2015. One thing it will not change is national inheritance tax.

### One inheritance law

All the Regulation does is apply one law to all your properties, even the properties in other countries. Normally, that will be the law of your last habitual residence. However, in your will you may choose the law of your country of nationality; the rules of that law will then apply to your entire succession.

*E.g.* *If you live in Belgium but have French nationality, Belgian law applies to your entire estate, including French real property and any property you have in another EU Member State. However, in your will you may decide that French law applies.*

The applicable law will decide who can inherit, whether you can disinherit your heirs or how much you have to reserve for them, how your heirs accept or waive an inheritance, whether they are liable for your debts under the succession, whether gifts have to be taken into account when determining what each heir inherits, and what wills are valid.

That law would also apply to the transmission of real property which is normally governed by the law of the country where the property is located. Nevertheless, local rules may apply for the acceptance or waiver of succession, and for the administration and liquidation of the succession. Of course, the state where the property is located may make the final transfer of the inheritance subject to the payment of inheritance taxes.

If you are not an EU national, you will also be allowed to choose the law of the country of your nationality. A US citizen living in Belgium could choose US American law. There is one condition: the laws of that country must be compatible with the values of equality and non-discrimination of the European Union. If you live in Belgium, the Belgian courts could disregard a foreign law if applying that rule would be contrary to public policy.

### The courts

Only the authorities in the deceased's habitual residence will have competence to settle the succession.

> In the example above, that would mean that the Belgian courts will have jurisdiction to rule in matters of successions and the heirs who want to accept or waive the succession would have to address the Belgian court.

If you have chosen French law to apply, the Belgian courts may defer the case to the French courts. If you have property in another country, the courts there may have to be involved.

### Certificate of Succession

The Regulation also introduces a European Certificate of Succession that must simplify and speed up the procedure. The certificate will constitute proof of the status of heir or legatee or of his powers as an administrator of the succession. That certificate will be recognised throughout the European Union.

Finally, court decisions and authentic deeds (notarised deeds) relating to successions will be more easily enforceable in the other Member States. They cannot impose additional conditions.

Once the regulation is implemented, on 17 August 2015, it should help avoid conflicts of law, reduce conflicts between heirs and simplify the administration of an estate.

One thing it will not solve is double taxation.

# INHERITANCE TAX ACROSS BORDERS

Potentially, one can face two types of inheritance tax problems in cross-border situations. First, there is the risk of taxation of a single inheritance by several states with no relief or only partial relief for double taxation. Moreover, they may also be exposed to tax discrimination in another country.

In most countries, the residence of the deceased is the sole criterion to charge inheritance tax. That is the case in Belgium. Belgium charges inheritance tax if either the deceased was a Belgian resident or, if he was not resident, inheritance tax will only be due on the real property he has in Belgium.

If a Belgian resident inherits from his parents living in another country, no Belgian inheritance tax will be due, even if inheritance tax is not due in the country where the deceased lived, where he was domiciled or where he had real property.

## Elimination of double taxation

If both countries have some sort of inheritance or estate tax, there may be a problem of double taxation.

Of course, if the country of domicile has abolished inheritance tax, there is no problem. If the deceased was domiciled in Austria, Cyprus, Estonia, Latvia, Malta, Portugal, Romania, the Slovak Republic, or Sweden, his heirs will only have to file a Belgian inheritance tax return for their Belgian real property.

How double taxation will be dealt with depends on the rules in the other country, Belgium only has a double tax treaty with France.

Most countries grant a credit for Belgian inheritance tax (Denmark, Finland, France, Germany, Ireland, Italy, Lithuania, the Netherlands, Spain, the U.K.). Some countries simply exempt the Belgian property from inheritance tax (the Czech Republic, Greece, Hungary, Slovenia) but some take account of the value of the Belgian property to calculate the tax rate on the assets that are liable to inheritance tax (this is the exemption-with-progression in the double tax treaty with France). A summary can be found at www.successions-europe.eu.

The table on p. 102 summarises the effective tax rates in selected EU Member States in 2010/2011 (Source : Press releases MEMO/11/917)

**Effective tax rates applicable in selected Member States in 2010/2011 (depending on availability)**

| Country | Remarks | The closest family (spouse and/or child) | | Non relatives | | Other remarks |
|---|---|---|---|---|---|---|
| | | € 50 000 | € 250 000 | € 50 000 | € 250 000 | |
| Austria | | | | | | Tax on land transfers and contribution to private foundations |
| Cyprus | | | | | | Tax on land transfers |
| Estonia | | | | | | Various fees |
| Latvia | | No inheritance tax | | | | |
| Malta | | | | | | Transfer duty |
| Romania | | | | | | Real estate tax |
| Slovakia | | | | | | |
| Sweden | | | | | | |
| Belgium | (Flanders) | 3.00% | 7.80% | 41.25% | 63.25% | |
| | (Walloon) | 3.50% | 9.70% | 46.25% | 71.25% | |
| | (Brussels) | 2.10% | 10.12% | 40.0% | 63.50% | |
| Bulgaria | | 0% | 0% | 0% | between 1.61% and 3.23% | Rates set by municipal authorities |
| Czech Republic | | 0% | 0% | 3.68% | 5.52% | |
| Denmark | spouse | 0% | 0% | 28.29% | 34.66% | |
| | child | 4.38% | 13.75% | | | |
| Finland | spouse | 0% | 8.16% | 13.40% | 28.04% | |
| | child | 5% | 11.28% | | | |
| France | spouse | 0% | 0% | 58.09% | 59.62% | |
| | child | | 6.54% | | | |
| Germany | | 0% | 0% | 3.60% | 27.60% | |
| Greece | spouse | 0% | 0% | 17.60% | 26.64% | |
| | child | 0% | 0.40% | | | |
| Hungary | spouse | 11.00% | 16.87% | 21.00% | 32.50% | |
| | child | 0% | 0% | | | |
| Ireland | | 0% | 0% | 14.65% | 22.93% | |
| Italy | | 0% | 0% | 8.00% | 8.00% | |
| Lithuania | | 0% | 0% | 4.71% | 9.88% | |
| Luxembourg | | 0% | 0% | 6.00% | 18.00% | |
| Netherlands | spouse | 0% | 0% | 28.79% | 34.93% | |
| | child | 6.18% | 13.72% | | | |
| Poland | | 0% | 0% | 19.06% | 19.81% | |
| Portugal | | 0% | 0% | 10.00% | 10.00% | Stamp duty upon death. Spouses and children are exempt. |
| Slovenia | | 0% | 0% | 15.20% | 20.68% | |
| Spain | | 0% | 0% | 6.16% | 15.55% | Assuming the pre-existing net assets of the heir do not exceed € 402 678.11 |
| UK | | 0% | 0% | 0% | 0% | A nil rate band applies up to GBP 325 000. Above this, the rate is 40% |

**Note:** For calculation purposes only lump sum allowances or general exemptions are included; personal tax deductions, such as those dependent on age or other special features are not accounted for. Effective tax rates may vary due to volatility of currency exchange rates.

We can distinguish the following potential double tax situations

# A Belgian resident has heirs abroad

In most countries the country of residence of the heir is irrelevant. Nevertheless, France, Germany, Poland and Spain charge inheritance tax if the heir lives there even if the deceased was a Belgian resident. That can result in double taxation, in Belgium and in the country where the heir or beneficiary lives.

### Relief by double tax treaty

For France, the problem is tackled with a tax treaty to avoid double inheritance tax. In accordance with the rules in this treaty, a French resident heir shall not have to file an inheritance tax return in France for real property outside France and he will not have to pay French inheritance tax.

### No Relief

Belgium does not have a double tax treaty with Germany and Spain to resolve problems of double inheritance tax.

Whether inheritance tax will be due in Spain depends on the autonomous community in which the heir lives, the national inheritance tax can go up to 34%, but some autonomous communities give quasi full exemptions (the Balearics, the Canary Islands, Murcia, Madrid, Valencia), although there may be restrictions on the amount inherited, or the recipient's prior wealth. In Andalucía, spouses and children are exempt if they inherit not more than €175,000, and do not have more than €402,678 in wealth.

In Germany, inheritance tax is a federal tax and the rules are the same. There is an exemption of €400,000 for children and €100,000 for anyone else.

### Relief in the other country?

If there is double inheritance tax, the other country may accept that the heir may deduct the Belgian inheritance tax from its own inheritance tax. It is, therefore, important to check whether and under which conditions there is such tax credit. Poland also charges inheritance tax when the heir lives in Poland but does not give any tax relief.

### Donate?

It may be possible to plan around this problem with a donation and pay gift tax in the country where the heir is living. If the donation is made before a local notary, that may meet the conditions to prove the date of the donation. In general, the donor will have to live for another three years to avoid Belgian inheritance tax.

# A Belgian resident has property abroad

Belgian inheritance tax is due on all your assets in Belgium and outside Belgium.

However, that property may also be liable to inheritance tax in that country as well. Moreover, if the heir lives in a country where he pays inheritance tax as well, there may be a case of triple taxation.

### Relief for real property

Belgium gives some relief for double taxation, but only for inheritance tax or estate tax that has been paid in the country where the real property is located. Foreign inheritance tax or estate tax due on real property in the other country can be deducted from the Belgian inheritance tax.

Foreign tax can only be credited if it has been paid. This means that there is no credit if the heirs do not pay inheritance tax in the other country or if they have an exemption of inheritance tax.

E.g.    *If a British couple has property in the U.K., they may have left it to each other in their wills, and between husband and wife no inheritance tax is due. They will still have to pay full inheritance tax in Belgium on the property in the U.K.*

The credit is calculated per heir and is limited to the part of the Belgian inheritance tax that corresponds to the foreign real estate calculated according to Belgian rules. That means that double taxation may not be entirely eliminated.

### Relief for movables

For movable assets, there is no such relief for double taxation, except for foreign estate tax, i.e. a tax that is levied on the estate as such (e.g. in the U.K., the executor pays the inheritance tax before he distributes the assets in the estate to the heirs).

Relief is not available for foreign inheritance tax on movables that is to be paid by the heirs personally. In practice, foreign estate tax is deducted from the value of the movables before the Belgian inheritance tax is calculated.

In most cases, this may result in double inheritance taxation, e.g. when a Belgian resident has investments on a Spanish bank account or if he holds shares of a German, a Greek or a US company.

### Plan around this problem with a donation?

This is possible: Belgian gift tax is only due on a donation of Belgian real property, but not on the donation of real property outside Belgium. Gift tax will probably be due there because real property needs to be transferred officially (e.g. before a notary). That will nevertheless be less than the inheritance tax that may be due in both countries. The three year rule would not even apply.

As for donations of movables, since these do not need to be passed before a Belgian notary, gift tax is not due in Belgium. The donor should stay alive for another three years.

## The deceased is not a Belgian resident

If the deceased was not resident in Belgium, no inheritance tax will be due in Belgium, unless he has real property in Belgium.

### Real property outside Belgium

Property outside Belgium is never liable to inheritance tax in Belgium.

### Real property in Belgium

If the deceased lived in another country, inheritance tax is due but only on his real property in Belgium; the inheritance tax is then called "tax on transfer upon death" (*recht van overgang bij overlijden / droit de mutation par décès*) but the same valuation rules and tax rates apply as for the regular inheritance tax.

However, no debts or liabilities may be deducted except for debts that have been specifically incurred in relation to the purchase or maintenance of these properties. In the Brussels Region and in Flanders, that is only the case if the deceased lived within the European Economic Area (that is the European Union, or Iceland, Liechtenstein or Norway).

Two (or more) inheritance tax returns will have to be filed: one in the country of domicile for the worldwide estate of the deceased, one in Belgium, for the real property he owned here and one in any other country where he has property or assets that are liable to inheritance tax there.

In Belgium, filing the inheritance tax return is an obligation for the heirs and the general legatees. If the deceased has appointed an executor in his will, or if the probate court has appointed an administrator, the executor or administrator may file the inheritance tax return.

The tax rate will be the rate applicable in the Brussels Capital region, in Flanders or Wallonia depending on the location of the property. If the deceased owned properties in different regions, it will be the region where the property with the highest cadastral revenue is located.

# Foreign nationals liable to inheritance tax at home

Some countries, such as the Netherlands, have anti avoidance rules to stop their nationals from leaving the country for tax purposes. In the case of the Netherlands, when a national of the Netherlands dies within 10 years following his emigration, he is deemed to be a resident of the Netherlands at the time of his death for the purposes of inheritance tax.

France considers introducing similar legislation to stop wealthy French nationals from leaving la douce France for tax reasons.

# U.S. citizens living in Belgium

The U.S. has similar rules. Even if U.S. citizens are resident in Belgium, their estate is liable to the federal estate tax applicable in the U.S. and possibly to a State estate tax.

However, that is usually a theoretical tax, since there are huge exemptions. According to the Tax Policy Center, just 3,800 estates will pay estate tax in 2013. Each U.S. citizen can make tax free bequests and donations for up to $5 million (indexed for inflation) and surviving spouses can claim any exemption not used by their deceased partners.

It is only if the estate is worth more than $5 million that estate tax will be due at a rate of 40%.

## Mismatches

Countries may also apply different rules because they do not see things the same way.

Tax transparent companies, like the French SCI, the *Société Civile Immobilière,* attract double taxation. It is treated as real property in France, but as movables in Belgium (the shares of the SCI); the double tax treaty obliges France to exempt the shares of the SCI.

A U.K. limited liability partnership would be considered a movable in Belgium, but it would qualify as a U.K. situs asset and be liable to U.K. inheritance tax if it is owned by a Belgian resident who is neither domiciled nor deemed domiciled in the U.K.

Usufruct is classified in Belgium as a valid gift or bequest of property which splits value. In the U.K., it is classified as a settlement within the relevant property regime for inheritance tax purposes and may give rise to an immediate charge to inheritance tax.

Life Insurance is another topic where the tax treatment differs largely from one jurisdiction to another.

# THE ART
# OF ESTATE PLANNING

Estate planning is about peace of mind for yourself. It is about making sure that your estate is used for what you want. That means that as your personal situation changes, you need to keep adjusting your plans.

Although estate planning is mostly assimilated with finding ways to minimise the tax, that should never be the first aim.

## ESTATE PLANNING, AN ART WITH MANY TOOLS

In the first place, estate planning is about making your assets last your lifetime and keeping assets in your estate with appropriate insurance, by minimizing the inheritance tax on your estate, and planning for the management of your finances and your medical care in case you become incapacitated and cannot manage them for yourself.

It is also about ensuring that your assets go to the people you choose, not those the state chooses. It is about making sure that your estate will go to whom you want and that their future is assured. In today's society with looser partnerships, blended or estranged families, that is getting more complicated. It is even more so in an international situation with property or heirs in another country.

If you have young children, estate planning is also planning for them if they were to lose both parents before adulthood. You can help the justice of the peace court designate the adult who will raise the children and manage their assets. If you don't, the justice of the peace will decide who will play those critically important roles in your children's lives.

Estate planning may also be about making sure that your children do not get your inheritance too early, or that they do not use it for the wrong purposes.

It is also about defusing potential family conflicts over your estate.

To a lesser degree, it is also about preparing a living will, a document that spells out the kinds of life-sustaining medical care you do and do not want if you are terminally ill or injured and close to death.

## The tools

The most obvious thing to do is draw up a will in which you give clear instructions about who gets what when you die. If inheritance tax is an issue, you may well want to start planning ahead and donate your possessions before your death. However, you can never foresee the future and you may want to anticipate accidents (e.g. that your children die before you). By making gifts you can avoid inheritance tax, we need to look at that as well before we can get to any form of estate and tax planning.

Changing your marriage contract can be a good piece of advice. Keep in mind that in Belgium, a marriage contract is not the same as a prenuptial agreement. Even if you have not signed a marriage contract or a prenup before you married, you can still change your marriage contract.

There are also different forms of contract that are used in Belgium to plan how your assets pass to your heirs, life insurance is an obvious choice. Finally, for some trusts and foundations may be a useful instrument.

## Checklist

**Do you know what is in your estate ?**
- Have you taken measures to maintain the value ?
- Is it adequately insured?
- Have you appointed a guardian?
- Do you have a living will?

**Who are your heirs and what will they get?**
- Your children / grandchildren
- Your spouse
- Your partner
- Your parents
- Your brothers and sisters
- Is that enough?

**Do you have any protected heirs?**
-	Your children / grandchildren
-	Your spouse
-	Your parents
	(you can disinherit your parents in favour of your spouse!)

**Will your protected heirs receive their fair share?**
-	Determine what your estate would be today
-	Have you made any donations that may be clawed back?
-	Calculate what your protected heirs are entitled to
-	Does your planning risk to cause controversy?
-	For all planning keep account of these limits

**Do you want to provide for your spouse ?**
-	Is a change of marriage contract advisable
-	A will can help within the disposable part
-	A donation? Revocation/Risk of clawback
-	Can you use your savings within an insurance policy?

**Do you want to provide for your children ?**
-	Are any living in another country?
-	Is a provision in your will sufficient?
-	If so, do you need to provide additional protection?
-	Do you want to give in advance?
-	If so, do you need to attach conditions to protect them?
-	Do you want to retain income?
-	Do you want to retain control?

**Do you want to provide for other relatives/friends ?**
-	Is a provision in your will sufficient?
-	How can you save on inheritance tax?

**Will your family find your will/instructions?**

# THE ART OF TAX PLANNING

Estate planning is mostly assimilated with finding ways to avoid paying inheritance or gift tax. Avoiding tax should never be the first and only reason for planning your estate, and that will become even more true in the future.

Whenever a new tax is introduced, someone somewhere will try and find a way to avoid paying the tax. Tax avoidance is not tax evasion. Tax evasion is refusing to pay the tax when it is due. Tax avoidance, on the contrary, is putting yourself in a situation where the tax is not due.

In Belgium, we call this "choosing the road of the lower taxation", and the Supreme Court has often repeated that it is allowed if only you accept all the consequences of that road. When you drive to the south, you can avoid the French motorway tax by taking the "routes nationales". The scenery is better but it will take you much longer to get there; there are more traffic lights and you cannot drive at 130km per hour. You can legally avoid the high tax on company cars, the road tax and the excise duties on petrol, by taking the train and the metro. If you do not want to pay the tax that a metro ticket is, you can take a bike. If you do not want to pay the bike tax ... we have not had a bike tax for a while, but you get the picture: it takes longer and you can get wet.

The taxman, however, does not like tax avoidance; it messes up the budget. That is why he came up with a general anti-abuse rule. Note that it is not a general anti-avoidance rule but an anti-abuse rule. That just confirms that you can still choose the road of the lower taxation, and if you do, you still have to accept all the consequences of that choice.

However, the tax authorities can now stop you from abusing your right to choose the road of the lower taxation. The law calls that "tax abuse"; if it was not the intention of the tax law that you set up a construction to pay less tax, the taxman can disregard the road of the lower taxation. To put it simply: the taxman can tell you that he thinks you have been too clever by half just to save tax.

If so, you have to convince the taxman that you had other valid reasons to choose that road. If you cannot convince him that the tax saving is just a happy coincidence, the taxman will make you pay the tax you thought you had so cleverly avoided.

A taxpayer can request an advance ruling from the Ruling Committee. That is a separate department within the tax administration. The committee is not authorized to decide that the tax administration will (or will not) apply the general anti-abuse rule or that a tax avoidance scheme is not abusive. Its role is limited to deciding whether a tax avoidance scheme (that may or may not be abusive) is justified by the non-fiscal motives of the taxpayer.

This anti-abuse rule has only been introduced in 2012 and we have not even started to see the extent of the grey area between tax avoidance and tax abuse.

What is worse: neither does the taxman.

In July 2012, the tax authorities gave us some clarification of what is acceptable and what is not acceptable. A number of simple and straightforward techniques are still acceptable: a hand-to-hand donation, a donation before a Dutch notary, bequeathing the family home to the surviving spouse to enjoy the exemption between husband and wife in Flanders, a donation with retention of usufruct, phasing a donation of real property over a period of time to benefit from the lower tax rates after three years and three days, generation skipping wills, a dual legacy, tontine and accruer clauses.

However, some complex or complicated techniques will be deemed to be abusive. The tax authorities have listed split purchase schemes (*usufruct / bare ownership* or *leasehold / freehold*), deathbed clauses in a marriage contract, changing a marriage contract to go for community property followed by a joint donation to the children by both spouses, or go for separation of properties followed by a reciprocal donation between husband and wife.

That does not mean that all of these transactions are definitively tax abuse; that depends on the situation and the circumstances. Even if a transaction is (potentially) an abusive tax avoidance scheme, the taxpayer may still justify it with other non-fiscal motives.

The new rule makes estate planning a bit more interesting but if you do not focus only on avoiding the tax, you should have nothing to worry about.

# SOME SIMPLE TECHNIQUES

In the following chapters we will look at how you can plan your estate with a will, by donating most of estate during your life, by changing your marriage contract, or using some other form of contract, such as a life insurance policy or even with a trust or foundation.

Saving on inheritance tax is, however, one of the main aims of estate planning and the following are some basic but drastic forms of estate planning.

## Spend it

You have no obligation to leave anything at all to your children or relatives. As long as you have made sure that they can fend for themselves, a popular piece of advice is "SKI", or "Spend the Kids' Inheritance".

That does not mean you can give it away, because that is a donation and your protected heirs, your children, could claw back any donations.

## Sell it

A sale is not a donation, unless you have agreed a ridiculously low price. However, if you sell, you receive a sales price and that will fall into your estate.

One way of avoiding that is to sell for an annuity and allow the purchaser to pay you a life annuity, that is reversible to your spouse or partner. A sale for a life annuity (*lijfrente / rente viagère*) is a technique that has become disused. Nevertheless, it can be a way of making sure that there is nothing left in your estate when you die.

Keep in mind that the reversion of the annuity may be a gift for your spouse or partner if they did not own the goods or the property you sell.

## Move

Because inheritance tax rules vary from one country to another, and from one region in Belgium to another, moving may be a useful option. There may be a higher nil rate band, lower inheritance tax rates, a different way of valuing the estate, etc ...

## Moving to another region within Belgium

Within Belgium, the Brussels Capital region, Flanders and Wallonia can determine what is in your estate and what is not, grant exemptions and lay down their own inheritance tax rates. Moving from one region to another may help save on inheritance tax.

Moving to Flanders may give you an exemption from inheritance tax on the family home between husband and wife and lower tax rates because the tax rates are calculated separately on real property and savings. A good spread of one's estate enables the heirs to benefit twice from the lower inheritance tax rates.

*E.g.* *A couple with a property worth €400,000 and savings worth €400,000 can leave that to their four children at a rate of 3%. Upon the first death the value of the assets is split over the surviving spouse and the children, but the surviving spouse does not pay tax on the usufruct on the house he inherits.*

*The share received by the children is worth less than €50,000 for the real property and less than €50,000 for the savings. Upon the second death, there is half a property worth €200,000 and savings worth €200,000, that is €50,000 and €50,000 per child so that they pay just 3%.*

If you plan to move to another region, try to make sure that you do that well in advance of your death. What is important is not the region where you lived but the region where you lived for the longest period of time in the last five years. If you moved from Brussels to an apartment at the coast two years before you die, inheritance tax will be due in Brussels. Moreover, it is not enough to register with the commune at your second residence, what counts is where you had your lived effectively.

## Moving to another country

Leaving Belgium may seem an attractive alternative. You can opt for another country that has a more favourable inheritance tax--, or more favourable succession rules.

In any event, a move needs to be a real move, you can keep a second residence in Belgium, but that must remain a second residence or you are just creating new problems of double domicile.

If you leave Belgium, the Belgian inheritance rules will no longer apply except for the real property you have here. You will be subject to the inheritance rules of the country to which you move. Whether a Belgian (or a foreign) will is to be considered valid in another country depends both on the legislation of the country where you live at the time of your death and on the legislation of the country where you have your assets. In any event, real property in Belgium will always be governed by the Belgian inheritance rules.

Moving to a common law country like the U.K. or the U.S. may also be a solution to get around the forced heirship rules. These countries do not stop you from disinheriting your children. However, you need to take proper advice; some countries refer back to your national law (that is called "renvoi") and may say that because you have Belgian or French nationality, the Belgian or French forced heirship rules will still apply.

Moreover, the U.K. may take the position that you have not taken up domicile in the Anglo Saxon sense.

Within the European Union, you can find some inspiration on www.successions-europe.eu. There is no inheritance tax in Austria, Cyprus, Estonia, Latvia, Malta, Portugal, the Slovak Republic and Sweden.

Some countries have low inheritance tax rates or large exemptions (Bulgaria, the Czech Republic, Estonia, Italy, Portugal, Romania).

Other countries do not charge inheritance tax between spouses or registered partner or between spouses and children (Bulgaria, the Czech Republic, Estonia, Ireland, Slovenia, the U.K.).

Most countries charge inheritance tax on the worldwide estate of the deceased if he was domiciled in the country. However, some countries have inverted that rule and charge inheritance tax if the heir lives in the country. That is the case for Spain. If you move to Spain and do not buy property there, keep your bank accounts in Belgium, your heirs will not pay inheritance tax in Spain, but they may have to pay inheritance tax in Belgium if you keep property here.

# PLAN IN YOUR WILL

Most Belgians do not draw up a will, the default intestate rules give them an acceptable solution. However, wills are used more and more frequently for estate planning to make sure your estate goes to who you wants, and to save on inheritance tax. People with larger estates are more likely to make a will since the tax rates are higher. Wills are most popular with people over 67, in particular if they are not married or do not have children.

There are three main reasons to draw up a will: to make sure that you decide who gets what, to attach conditions to your will which make it easier to enforce, or to pay less inheritance tax.

## YOU DECIDE WHO GETS WHAT

If you want to change the default inheritance rules, you need to make a will. You can decide that some of your relatives get more. If you want to look after your partner financially and you have not registered the partnership, you have no alternative but to make a will. If you want to leave something to charity, you can do so with a will as well.

The only thing you have to take account of is the forced heirship rules that do not allow you to disinherit your children and grandchildren and your spouse entirely. It is only if you have no forced heirs that you can leave everything to whoever you want.

### Change the default order of succession

The first use of a will is to change the default order of inheritance as defined by law (see p. 28). If you are not happy with the solution offered by law, you can change it by making a will (within the limits of the forced heirship rules that protect your children and spouse).

*E.g.    Jonathan never married and has no children. His only relatives are his sisters Maud and Maureen. Each has a son: Ralph and Frédéric. Frédéric is also Jonathan's godson. If he does not make a will, Maud and Maureen will inherit his entire estate and divide it in two. Jonathan may want to favour his godson, and he can do that by appointing Frédéric as his legatee in his will and leave him everything.*

*His sisters cannot do anything about that, they are not protected heirs.*

You cannot disinherit your children and spouse completely (see p. 49). However, you can disinherit your husband if you are separated. Even then he still inherits from you in the first six months of your separation or, afterwards if you have not excluded him in your will. You must formalise the separation through the courts and you must live for another six months after you separate. And if he moves in with you again, then the separation does not count.

## Decide who gets what

You may not want to change the normal order of inheritance, but you may want to determine who gets what exactly. If you do not make a will, your heirs will receive all your assets together and they will have to distribute them amongst themselves. A wine cellar can be divided, a collection of books can be split up with a bit more difficulties, but there are things that you cannot share. Take a moment to think about how your children will be fighting amongst themselves about your favourite painting, a piece of furniture, an old-timer, ...

They will always find a solution but often with many bad feelings. You may want to tell them that it is your decision to leave your collection of watches to Jonathan and your mother's jewellery to Elise. A will can be used to distribute some or all of your assets to prevent family feuds. From a psychological point of view, children tend to accept the solution imposed by their parents more easily than they do if they have to work it out themselves. Keep in mind they can always swap amongst themselves.

A will can also be used to make sure that the family business is inherited by one child rather than another, but usually it is advisable to plan that well in advance.

## Help one or more of your children

Parents may also want to favour one or more of their children out of a sense of equity. You may want to acknowledge that life is not fair and that some of your children were not as successful or lucky in their professional career. When Mick Jagger's father Joe died in 2006, at the age of 93, he left all of his assets not to Mick but to his other son Chris, whose career as a musician never hit the same heights. Of course, Joe

Jagger would never have been able to disinherit his son if he was living in Belgium, but there is part of your estate, the disposable estate, that you can give to whoever you want.

Redistributing your assets in your will may also be a way of helping children with a physical or mental disability. Or it can compensate a child who has been working in the family business for a low salary.

If you do not feel comfortable treating your children differently, it is advisable to explain in your will why you are doing it. Of course, it is always better to talk to family members and explain why you want to leave your money elsewhere. I assume that is what Joe Jagger had done, Mick Jagger was named as his father's executor.

Finally, you can also use your will to punish one or more of your heirs. If the relation with one of your heirs (a child, a sibling, ...) has become troubled, you may want to disinherit them, even partially. Again, this is something that you need to think through. This may be a recipe for lengthy court proceedings and bad feelings between your heirs.

## Help your spouse

Making a will in favour of your spouse is not the most appropriate solution; more can be achieved with a marriage contract or with other contractual arrangements (see hereinafter). Nevertheless a will can help to give each other a bit more. A lot depends on your situation and your matrimonial property regime.

If you have children, your spouse will normally inherit the usufruct in your estate. We have seen what the consequences and drawbacks are. You can deny your heirs the right to ask for the conversion of that usufruct to give your spouse a bit more control. Alternatively, if you anticipate that one of your children is going to make difficulties for your wife, you can give her the maximum you can so that she keeps control over more assets.

E.g.   *Aristea and Stephen have always lived in Belgium since they were married, their family assets are community property. When Aristea dies, Stephen only inherits the usufruct of Aristea's share of the community property, while their children inherit the bare ownership. The apartment Aristea inherited from her parents in Brussels is her separate property and will be inherited by the children with an usufruct for Stephen. Because he only has the usufruct, Stephen cannot sell the property. Aristea may want to draw up a will to give him full ownership.*

If you have no children, there is one rule you need to know about. Your parents inherit together with your brothers and sisters (and their descendants): in that case each parent receives one quarter – the rest (1/2 or 3/4) is distributed between the siblings). You can disinherit your siblings in favour of anyone. However, you can only disinherit your parents by making a will in favour of your spouse.

## Look after your partner

If you want to do something for your partner, you have no alternative but to make a will. Unless you register your partnership, your partner does not inherit anything from you. In addition, a registered partner only inherits the usufruct on the family home (if his partner owned it) as well as the furniture in the family home. If you want to leave your partner more, you have to draw up a will. Even then, you can disinherit your registered partner; he is not a forced heir.

## Make bequests

If you have no heirs or only very distant relatives, you are well advised to make a will just to help the people who deal with your estate find out who will inherit. With families spread over the entire world, it is not uncommon that someone dies with nieces and nephews on other continents. If they cannot be tracked down, your estate goes to the Belgian State.

If that is a risk, you may want to make bequests to a good friend or to a charity or your old university. These are not just Belgian charities or institutions. You can leave small sums of money to friends or relatives, or to charities even if you have children or a spouse – keep in mind that you must not exaggerate; they are your protected heirs.

Another important thing to remember is that the beneficiary will have to pay inheritance tax at the rate depending on their relationship to you. If they are not related to you and there are many of them, the inheritance tax rates can be quite high, although there are some reduced rates for charities and organisations in Belgium or in the European Economic Area.

## Appoint a general legatee

If you have no direct relatives, or if you have only one or two children living in Belgium, it may be advisable to appoint someone as your general legatee. You can leave everything to that beneficiary and he can administer your estate, a bit like an executor or administrator following probate. It may make the administration and the filing of the inheritance tax return easier.

Even if you have forced heirs, you can appoint a general legatee to whom you leave everything. He will inherit everything but with an obligation to give an equal share to his siblings.

The risk that the general legatee has to pay the inheritance tax is also a guarantee that the inheritance tax will be paid out of the estate.

## ATTACH CONDITIONS TO YOUR WILL

Not only can you decide who gets what in your will, you can make your bequests subject to certain conditions. There are all sorts of conditions and obligations you can impose on your heirs and legatees. In fact, a bequest is an obligation you impose on your heirs to give something to someone else. You can oblige your heirs to give a car or a painting to a friend, but you can also oblige them to pay a monthly annuity to your spouse, your partner or the person who has been looking after you.

You can also ask them to look after your cat. Janis Joplin posthumously organised an all-night party for 200 guests at her favourite pub in San Anselmo, California, "so my friends can get blasted after I'm gone." You can be as creative as you want...

## Control your estate from the grave

If you are a parent or a grandparent and you want to leave something in your will to a young child or a grandchild, it is normal that you want to make sure that they use it well. When is a child mature enough to have money? 25? 30? 40? Someone told me once "my children get nothing until they are 40; I do not want to rob them of the chance of an education."

Since you hold the strings, you decide. You may even decide that they get a quarter at 25, and another quarter at 30, 35 and 40.

How do you control the money until they reach that age?

### A delayed bequest

In common law countries, like the U.K., the solution would be to put the inheritance in an accumulation trust and to give the trustee clear instructions about when he can give what and to whom. We do not have trusts in Belgium (see p. 173), your children inherit your estate and automatically become the full owners upon your death even if they are minor, they just are supervised by their guardian, until they reach adulthood at 18.

Can you put a condition in your will that someone you trust will have the right to manage your estate until your children have a certain age and will release the assets in stages? That would give the children the ownership of your estate but they would not be able to use it. While this is well organised in e.g. the Netherlands, it is a bone of contention in Belgian law; there is no provision in the law that allows it, but there is also none that forbids it. Moreover, there is no case law and you do not want have some case law named after you.

That means that such a provision in your will could be attacked by your children. In particular, they could state that they are protected heirs and that they must receive their forced share free and without any limitations. Imposing such supervision would impinge on their forced share, and the children could ask the court to declare it null and void. However, you could hope that they will just accept your wishes; if they go to court, that may take some time, maybe until they reach the minimum age you have put in your will.

### Extended guardianship

There are specific provisions in the law about the management of an estate by a guardian of minors or mentally disabled children. These provisions make it difficult to sell the estate until the youngest child is 18. You can extend the powers of the guardian past 18 with a provision in your will that gives the guardian the right to manage and control your estate until the youngest of your children reaches a certain age, say 25 or 30.

That would limit the children in their freedom to sell the properties but not completely. When they are all 18, they could try and overturn these powers by simply agreeing to sell the properties. Since the guardian's powers of management are an obligation rather than a right

124

for the guardian, he may have difficulties defending your wishes, except maybe for the disposable part of your estate!

There are any number of imaginative solutions to deal with this, depending on your situation and the nature of the assets in your estate. You can give the guardian an usufruct over your assets, you can give him a lifelong rental contract on your property or properties for a peppercorn rent, you could rent out the properties with a right of first refusal for the tenant if your heirs want to sell the property. Or you can do what Bernard Arnault, the CEO of the LVMH group did, he set up a private foundation to block the division of his empire until 2023 when his youngest will be 25.

## The carrot and the stick

If you are worried that your heirs will create problems, there are a few ways of enforcing these conditions in your will.

You can include a penalty in your will, and if your heirs refuse to enforce the will, take away the bequest or limit their right to inherit the estate. If you have two children, they must each receive a third of your estate; that means you have a hold over them for the remaining third: "if you do not respect my wishes you only inherit a third, and the rest will go to your brother who respects my wishes or to X (*think of someone they really dislike*)".

Another solution is to make an alternative bequest. You give your heir two choices. In a first bequest he gets more than he must receive by law, but then he must comply with a condition or a charge linked to his bequest.

Alternatively, he just receives the minimum he is entitled to without any condition or charge. If he opts for the first bequest, he is rewarded for respecting your will.

## A pass through bequest

Another way of controlling your estate is a pass through bequest (there are pass through donations as well). This allows you to decide not once but twice who receives your estate. In your will you appoint the first beneficiary; he receives the estate immediately upon your death and he owns it until he dies. What is left upon his death will then be inherited by the second beneficiary you have appointed in your will (or in the donation).

This requires some careful planning. This is substitution and substitution is forbidden because it is reminiscent of the feudal system abolished by the French Revolution. Substitution is the obligation for the beneficiary to keep the assets intact and to pass them on to a designated third party. It is forbidden except if the obligation is imposed on your child or on your brother and sister in order to pass the gift or bequest on to their own child(ren).

Note that it is this obligation in the will or donation to pass the assets intact that is the problem. If anyone (including the tax authorities) petitions the court, the court can declare the obligation unwritten but that would not necessarily have any effect on the other provisions of the donation or will.

What is not a problem is the obligation to pass on what is left over on the first beneficiary's death. That is called *"fideicommissio de residuo"*. The difference with substitution is that the first beneficiary is not obliged to keep the estate intact, he can sell or give away.

This can be useful for a couple that does not have any children and wants to provide for each other without disinheriting their own family. Upon the death of the surviving husband, the property he inherited from his wife will revert to his wife's nieces and nephews.

This also allows the wife to make sure that the assets in her estate stay in her family (her nieces and nephews) and do not go to her husband's family. In fact, it can also be used to prevent a son or daughter in law from inheriting the usufruct of family assets by imposing an obligation on the daughter or son to pass on the asset to the (existing) grandchild(ren) or to a brother or sister.

This can also be used by grandparents who give something to their children with the obligation to pass it on to their children.

Finally, this also allows people with a disabled child to reward the person who will care for their child after their own death. The child is the first beneficiary, the carer the second.

We will explain hereafter how this may be tax efficient.

# WRITE A TAX EFFICIENT WILL

## Leave the family home to your spouse

In Flanders, and only if you are resident in Flanders, there is no inheritance tax between husband and wife. If they leave each other their share in the family home, they will save on inheritance tax.

However, you must make sure that the children, if there are any, get their forced share, or you have to compensate for that with some sort of claim for the children *vis-a-vis* their parent. Moreover, in Flanders, the inheritance tax is calculated separately for the real property and the other possessions.

## Spread your inheritance

If you leave everything to one person, he will pay inheritance tax at the higher rates. By spreading the inheritance over a large number of people, each of them will pay tax on a smaller inheritance.

*E.g.*  *If you leave your two children, Sara and Felipe, they will each pay inheritance tax on half. If you leave them €600,000, they will pay inheritance tax on €300,000 each. In Flanders that will be €33,000 each, or €66,000 in total. If you make a will that gives €150,000 to Sara and €150,000 to her son, and €100,000 to Felipe and €100,000 to his two children, each of them pays inheritance tax at the lower tax rates. Sara and her son pay €10,500 each; Felipe and his children pay €6,000 each. The tax saving will be €27,000 (€66,000 - €39,000).*

That is usually a good idea because the children, Sara and Felipe, are well off, and the grandchildren are the ones that could use a little help to buy their first house.

Keep in mind that if you spread your inheritance by leaving a sum of money to friends and relatives, they will pay inheritance tax at the higher rates. If they are in a category of heirs where the tax rate is calculated on what everyone in the group inherits (see the rates for Brussels or Flanders), spreading your inheritance in that group will not help.

# Skip a generation

The example above with the grandchildren is a form of generation skipping. That results in a double tax saving. There is a saving by spreading the inheritance, but by skipping a generation, one also saves inheritance tax upon Sara's or Felipe's death. When granddad leaves his possessions to his son, who, in turn, will leave them to his own son, inheritance tax will be due twice, upon granddad's death and upon dad's death. That means that when granddad makes a bequest to his grandson directly, no inheritance tax is due upon dad's death.

The problem may be that Sara and Felipe feel left out. Why should they have to share with their children? Why can they not inherit everything? Moreover, they are forced heirs and under the forced heirship rules, they should get two thirds of granddad's estate. If that is €600,000, they should get €200,000 each. Of course, if Sara and Felipe do not mind, there is no problem; only they can attack the will. And they may see the benefit.

### Variation #1

If you fear that your children will object, you can use a first variation. In your will you can give the grandchildren the bare ownership and the children the usufruct. You can also leave everything to the grandchildren with an obligation for them to pay a regular income (e.g. 4 or 5% interest) to their parents.

### Variation #2

A second variation is called granddad's or grandma's will (*"ik-opa"* *testament / testament de grand-père*). Granddad leaves everything to the children with an obligation for them to acknowledge a debt to their children that will be payable at the latest at their own death. That means the grandchildren inherit an I.O.U. from their grandfather or grandmother; they will pay inheritance tax on that receivable, but on a discounted value of what they will receive at their own parents' death.

It achieves the aim of spreading the inheritance tax over more beneficiaries (children and grandchildren) and of skipping inheritance tax on father's or mother's death. If Sara or Felipe pay off their debt before they die, that money will not be in their estate anymore. If they have not, that I.O.U. can be deducted from the estate when calculating the inheritance tax on their estate.

This technique is considered to be aggressive by the tax authorities. If you chose for this, make sure you are probably advised.

## A will for a single person with no children

When the deceased has no partner or children, his estate is inherited by his parents and siblings. The inheritance tax rate between siblings is much higher than between parent(s) and descendants.

It will save inheritance tax if the person in question leaves everything to his parent(s) who can then leave it to his siblings. The estate is inherited twice at the reduced tax rates between parents and children. First at the reduced rates between the son and his parents, and then between the parents and their (other) children.

## Make a pass through bequest

A pass through bequest is a bequest where you appoint the first beneficiary of your estate as well as the next beneficiary who will receive the estate on the death of the first. Not all pass through bequests are allowed.

A pass through bequest is a double bequest and inheritance tax will be due twice. Inheritance tax on the second transfer will be the rate applicable at the time of the first death as if the bequest in the will was made directly to the second beneficiary. The value of the bequest will be calculated on the day of the first beneficiary's death. That will have an effect on a pass through bequest imposed on a brother or sister. The inheritance tax rate will be determined for a bequest to a nephew or niece, and not as the rate for descendants (between the brother and his child). A pass through donation may, therefore, be more efficient.

## Leave something to a charity

A tax efficient way of planning your estate is to give to a charity.

Charities, as well as non profit associations, international associations and foundations, pay inheritance tax at a fixed rate of 7% if the deceased lived in Wallonia, 8.8% if he lived in Flanders and 25% if he lived in Brussels (in Brussels non-profit associations that may issue tax certificates for donations pay 12.5%).

The beneficiary must not be a Belgian organisation; usually all non profit associations, international associations and foundations qualify if they are set up in the European Economic Area.

## The dual legacy: a clever bequest

A bequest to a charity can also be a way of reducing the inheritance tax rate for your heirs, in particular if they are distant relatives or relations.

This is a useful tip if you have no partner or children. If you live in Wallonia and leave €500,000 to a foundation, the rate is 7% and the foundation will receive €465,000. If you leave your shares worth €500,000 to a foundation and your house worth €500,000 to your niece Ineta "free of inheritance tax" (*the wording is important*), Ineta will receive the house and will not have to pay any inheritance tax.

The foundation will pay the inheritance tax for Ineta, that is €309,750. It will also pay its own inheritance tax, €70,000. The foundation will have €155,250 left and Ineta has the house. If she had inherited the shares and the house, the tax would have €659,375; she would have had to sell the shares and still find €159,375 to keep the house. A lot of hassle and chances are she would have no alternative but to sell the house.

The technique can be effective for smaller bequests. If you live in Flanders and leave €25,000 to a friend, he pays 45% inheritance tax and keeps €13,750. If you leave €15,000 to a friend "free of inheritance tax" and €10,000 to a non-profit association, there will be less inheritance tax. Your friend keeps €15,000 and the association pays 45% inheritance tax of €15,000 (for the friend), that is €6,750 and 8.8% on €10,000, that is €880. The association keeps €2,370.

This can also work for closer relatives; it is a question of doing the maths. For descendants, it can reduce the inheritance tax if the estate is worth over €250,000.

This technique is called a *duo-legaat / legs en duo*. What you are doing, in fact, is appointing the charity as your general legatee, and the charity has to administer your estate. If you want your relative or friend to remain in control, you can leave everything to your relative or friend as a general legatee with an obligation to give a large part of the estate to a charity subject to the charity accepting the pay the inheritance tax for the first beneficiary.

*Duo-legaat* / *legs en duo* is becoming big business, and some charities are specialising in them. Just google *duo-legaat* or *legs en duo*. If they are open to administer your estate for a bequest, they will usually mention that on their website. Keep in mind that they prefer cash to real property; it is far less hassle for the charity.

Moreover, you must leave a substantial part of your estate to the charity or the dual legacy may be seen as aggressive tax planning.

# PLAN BY DONATING

The most tax efficient form of tax planning is to give everything away during your lifetime. If you have nothing left, and you have made sure that your protected heirs have received their share so that they do not need to claw back life time donations, you have successfully planned your estate and your heirs will not pay any inheritance tax.

However, that is not really an option for you and that is why we have an entire chapter on estate planning through donations.

## HOW DO YOU DONATE?

In Belgian law, a donation is a contract between a donor and a beneficiary. The donor gives something away and the beneficiary accepts it, but what is important is that the donor must have the intention to give away, for good, and without expecting anything back.

Between donor and beneficiary, a good understanding is sufficient; nothing else is needed.

It is only when a third party becomes involved that one has to prove that the gift was a donation. The children may contest that dad had given a large sum of money to his new partner.

The taxman may have difficulties with donations as well; they are too effective to avoid inheritance tax.

### Before a Notary?

The civil code states that for a donation to be valid, a lifetime donation must be recorded in a notarised deed. The donation and the acceptance of the donation are then registered in an authentic deed. The notary arranges for registration of that deed and at that occasion gift tax is due (see p. 132).

The benefit of a notarised deed is that the content and the date of that deed cannot be contested. The only thing the heirs can do is get the donation cancelled if the donor has given more than he could under the forced heirship rules (see p. 49).

However it is generally accepted that assets can be donated by way of a hand-to-hand donation (see p. 137) or by a bank transfer (see p. 140). Nevertheless, a donation of real property must always be made in front of a notary.

Moreover, you may want the security of a notarised deed; it allows you to attach conditions to your donation, or maybe you do not have three years left and gifts in the last three years are liable to inheritance tax. The safe option then is to donate before a notary, and that triggers gift tax.

# Gift tax

Gift tax is a registration tax (*registratierecht / droit d'enregistrement*) that is due when a document that establishes a donation is registered in Belgium with the Ministry of Finance. All notarial documents must be registered irrespective of their content.

A donation of real property located in Belgium must always be made in the form of a notarial deed and will always be liable to gift tax. Donations of real property located outside Belgium must not be registered in Belgium and are exempt from gift tax, at least in Belgium.

Donations of movables (cash, shares, portfolio, ...) must not be passed before a notary and private donation agreements must not be registered. Registration is not required and, therefore, we can say that gift tax on movables is optional. However, if the donor makes a donation before a Belgian notary, gift tax is due (at a flat rate of 3 or 7%, see below).

In theory, gift tax is due by the beneficiary. In practice, the gift tax is to be paid to the notary who draws up the gift deed, as he will be paying the gift tax to the taxman. Either the donor or the beneficiary can pay the gift tax to the notary and if the donor pays the tax, that will not be considered to be part of the donation.

## Cross border donations

A Belgian residence is irrelevant to determine whether gift tax is due in Belgium. Gift tax is due when a document is registered that shows a donation even if that is a donation between two non-residents.

That also means that no Belgian gift tax is due when a donation is passed before a foreign notary, but local gift tax may be due in that country. That is why a donation before a Dutch or Swiss notary is an often used tax planning technique.

Whether gift tax is due in Belgium or not, some countries charge gift tax if the beneficiary is living there. A beneficiary living in Spain will have to pay gift tax (*impuesto sobre donaciones*) and if he receives real property or securities in Belgium, he will have to declare these to the national *Agencia Tributaria Estatal*.

Beneficiaries in France, Germany and Poland face the same problem but these countries have important exemptions and they may allow a set off of Belgian gift tax against their own gift tax.

If, on the contrary, the donor lives in Spain, and the beneficiary lives in Belgium, Spain does not levy gift tax unless real property or movables located in Spain are donated.

## Brussels, Flanders or Wallonia?

The applicable law (between that of the Brussels, Flemish or Walloon Regions) is determined by the tax residence of the donor, even for property located in another region. If he had moved recently from another region, gift tax will be due in the region where he lived the longest in the last five years.

If the donor is not a Belgian resident in Belgium, the donation will be governed by the legislation of the region where the property is located and for a donation of movables, the region where the notary is established.

## How is gift tax calculated?

Gift tax is calculated on the value of the things that you give, that is the fair market value without any deductions for obligations imposed on the beneficiary. There are a few exceptions.

Securities listed on the stock exchange are valued on the basis of the list published every month by the tax authorities in the Belgian Official Journal; the value is the value in the latest listing.

Usufruct (see p. 59) on real property is valued by multiplying the annual rent or return with the coefficient in the table on p. 79, depending on the age of the person to whom you give the usufruct. If that person is 64, the gift tax will be due on 38% of the value of the property in question.

If you give a usufruct for e.g. ten years, it is valued by capitalizing the annual return or the rent at 4%; the maximum value is the value for a lifetime usufruct or 80% of the value of the property.

If the usufruct is linked to the life of more than one person, only the age of the beneficiary who receives the usufruct must be taken into account.

The value of bare ownership is the value of the full ownership less the value of the usufruct.

There is one important exception.

if the donor gives a property away and keeps the usufruct for himself, gift tax is due on the full value of the property; he cannot take a deduction for the usufruct he retains

## Gift tax rates

The gift tax rates depend from one region to another. The gift tax rate are similar to the inheritance tax rates, but there is a flat rate for the donation of movables.

### Movables

The gift tax on **movables** is 3% between (grand)parents and (grand)children and between spouses and registered partners, and 7% for all other donations.

In Wallonia, however, the rates are 3.3% and 7.7% with an intermediate rate of 5.5% in Wallonia for donations between brothers and sisters and between uncles or aunts and nephews or nieces.

### Real property

The gift tax rates on **real property** are progressive. Gift tax it is calculated depending on the region and the degree of kinship between the donor and the beneficiary. The rates are as follows in the direct line and between spouses and registered partners.

Brussels

| On the band between | | | Rate | Tax on previous bands |
|---|---|---|---|---|
| €0 | - | €50 000 | 3% | |
| €50 000 | - | €100 000 | 8% | + €1 500 |
| €100 000 | - | €175 000 | 9% | + €5 500 |
| €175 0000 | - | €250 000 | 18% | + €12 250 |
| €250 000 | - | €500 000 | 24% | + €25 750 |
| over €500 000 | | | 30% | + €85 750 |

Flanders and Wallonia

| On the band between | | | Rate | Tax on previous bands |
|---|---|---|---|---|
| €0 | - | €12 500 | 3% | |
| €12 500 | - | €25 000 | 4% | + €375 |
| €25 000 | - | €50 000 | 5% | + €875 |
| €50 000 | - | €100 000 | 7% | + €2 125 |
| €100 000 | - | €150 000 | 10% | + €5 625 |
| €150 000 | - | €200 000 | 14% | + €10 625 |
| €200 000 | - | €250 000 | 18% | + €17 625 |
| €250 000 | - | €500 000 | 24% | + €26 625 |
| over €500 000 | | | 30% | + €86 625 |

The rates for all other beneficiaries can be found in the annexes on p.235).

Note that successive donations of Belgian real property may be added up to calculate the gift tax rate. When real property is donated within three years of a previous donation of real property, the value of the previous donation is added to the value of the subsequent donation.

## Gift tax or Inheritance tax?

The most important reason for making a donation is to save on inheritance tax. Of course, if you can avoid paying gift tax, that is an added bonus.

However, how do gift tax and inheritance tax work together?

Usually, if you pay Belgian gift tax, your heirs will not pay inheritance tax on what you have given, not even if the beneficiary must give back what has been given upon the donor's death because he has given more than he should have under the forced heirship rules.

However, if you have made a donation in the last three years before your death, the tax authorities will add all donations in the last three years before the donor's death to his estate to calculate the inheritance tax rate due on his estate; that just means that the inheritance tax may be a bit higher.

But what if you have made a tax free donation? The good news is that it is not because gift tax has not been paid that inheritance tax will be due. That is where the three year rule kicks in. The three year rule means that anything given in the last three years of one's life is added to the value of his estate and will be subject to inheritance tax if no gift tax has been paid.

In other words, by giving something away during your lifetime, you can avoid both gift tax and inheritance tax; you just have to live for another three years after the donation. That is why a hand to hand donation or a donation from one bank account to another or even a donation before a Dutch or Swiss notary are popular estate planning techniques, the only proviso is that the donor must live for another three years after the donation.

## MAKE A TAX EFFICIENT DONATION

Just like with wills, there are three reasons to make a donation.

Making sure that the beneficiary receives what you want is an easy one: you give to whom you want, all you have to do is take account of the forced heirship rules.

Most donors also opt for a donation because they want to save on tax. If the beneficiary has to wait until you die, inheritance tax will be due. If the donation is made long enough before you die, no inheritance tax will be due and there are ways of donating without gift tax.

Saving tax is what all donors want but it requires giving now rather than later, and most donors are not ready to let go. That is why we will look at a number of ways to keep some form of control over your donation.

### Donate before a notary

If you want to donate movables, you can make a donation before a notary at a very low rate: between 3 and 7%, or, in Wallonia, 3.3%,

5.5% or 7.7%. However, that gift tax is optional because you can opt to donate without going to a notary.

If you want to donate real property, you have no alternative but to do so before a Belgian notary, and the rates are about the same as the inheritance tax rates. However, gift tax does not have the reduced inheritance tax rates for the main residence and there are no tax savings for retaining the usufruct (the right to live in the property or to collect the rent). If you donate real property and retain usufruct, gift tax is, nevertheless, calculated on the full market value of the property. That tax is due now, rather than upon your death, but you can finance it yourself.

### Spread the donation over time

Every donation of real property is calculated starting in the lower tax brackets. By spreading the donation over separate donations of a percentage of the property, you can use the lower tax brackets several times as long as you wait three years and a few days between donations.

Indeed, it is only when real property is donated within three years of a previous donation of real property, that the value of the previous donation is added to the value of the present donation.

*That means that a person living in Brussels can make a donation of a portion of his property every three years (plus a couple of days) for a value of up to €50,000 per child and only pay 3% gift tax. If he has three children, he can give €150,000 every three years. The rate is 5.5% on €300,000, and 6.67% on €450,000.*

In Flanders and Wallonia, the rates are a bit higher.

*On €50,000 (per child), the rate is 4.25%, on €100,000 (per child) the rate is 5.625, and on €150,000 (per child) it is 7.08%.*

With the prices of properties in Brussels nowadays, it might take a while before you transfer the full property. What is more, every three years, the value of the properties goes up but the brackets are not index linked.

# The hand to hand donation

Although the law states that a donation must be made before a notary, that is only the theory. A hand-to-hand donation (*handgift / don manuel*) is legally valid. All that is required is that the gift is literally handed over into the hands of the beneficiary. In Belgium, ownership of movables is proven by possession.

The important thing is to prove that the donation was made more than three years before the death of the donor; if he does not live for another three years, the donation will be added to his estate and inheritance tax will be due.

### Disadvantages

Hand-to-hand donations have a few limitations. You can only hand over assets that you can handle. You cannot hand over real property, intangible rights such as a copyright, or shares or bonds that are registered in a share register or a register of bonds with the company issuing the shares or bonds.

Until a few years ago, most Belgian companies issued bearer shares or bearer bonds and these could easily be handed over. As they were the favourite tool for estate planners, they have been made illegal.

A second problem is that a hand-to-hand donation is still difficult to prove. If dad's girlfriend shows off grandmother's diamonds at his funeral, how do the children know that dad had given them and that not she has not taken them out of his safe?

Finally, a hand-to-hand donation is made without any written contract. It is difficult to attach any conditions (see p. 144).

### How to do a hand-to-hand donation?

To give money by way of a hand-to-hand donation, you need to hand over the money. That is not very convenient for large amounts of money, just imagine bringing a couple of millions home in your briefcase. I am not even sure that the bank would be too pleased to see you leave with this amount of money.

The only practical way to do that is to organise for the bank to have the amount of cash available at a given date, to invite the beneficiary to the branch of the bank at that date, to take the money out of your account and hand it over to the beneficiary in front of the bank manager. The beneficiary then puts the money on his own bank account.

How do you do this? Keep in mind that we need to set up a paper trail to prove that the donation was made more less than three years before the death of the donor.

### Step by step

Let us take the example of Nancy and her daughter Francine. A hand to hand donation takes some planning: Nancy has to make sure that the branch has sufficient cash in house on a date that suits both her and Francine.

First, Nancy addresses a registered letter to her daughter inviting her to meet her at the branch of her bank on such and such a date, at a certain time, because she wants to make a donation. The letter is meant to show Nancy's intention to gift. The registered letter must prove the date of the letter. One can send the letter with a return receipt message (*ontvangstbewijs / accuse de reception*). This is a pink form that is attached to the registered letter, to be signed by Francine for receipt and returned to Nancy.

The postmark should be put on the letter itself. A postmark on the envelope only proves that an envelope was sent; it might have contained a blank letter. Use a piece of A3 paper (that is the double of an A4), you fold it in two and then in three. When you write on the inside half, the outside half becomes the envelope. You can seal that with scotch tape on the three open sides. The post office will put the postmark on the stamp on the outside part of the piece of paper and that cannot be separated from the letter.

On the agreed date, Nancy and Francine meet with the bank manager. He takes the money out of Nancy's account, makes her sign a receipt and gives it to her. Nancy pushes the money to Francine's side of the table. Francine is now the official owner of the money and she can put it on an account she has opened previously with the bank. That money has been taken out from Nancy's account and put on Francine's account.

Finally, Francine sends a thank you letter to her mother, thanking her for the donation of the money. The format of the letter should be the same as above (A3). A model of the letters can be found in the annexes.

The donation is proven with the two registered letters, the bank statements showing the money is going off Nancy's account and arriving on Francine's bank account, the receipts signed by Nancy when she received the money from the bank and the document signed by Francine and the bank manager when she deposits the money.

It goes without saying that Francine must keep a file with the two original letters, a copy of the statements showing that the money has left Nancy's account and have arrived on her own account, together with the receipts.

A hand-to-hand donation is used most commonly to give cash, but it can also be used for securities like stocks and bonds that Nancy has on her account with the bank.

## A donation by bank transfer

It is more practical to transfer the money or the securities (such as stocks or bonds) from one bank account to another. That is not a hand-to-hand donation between donor and beneficiary but an "indirect donation" in legal slang. The donation passes from the donor to beneficiary via the bank.

For a long time, lawyers have been disagreeing whether this was a valid alternative for a hand-to-hand donation. The Minister of Finance has now confirmed that such donation is valid even if the donation does not pass before a notary

### Disadvantages

Bank-to-bank donations are limited to assets that can be recorded on a bank account and transferred from one bank account to another. It is not possible for real property or copyright.

A bank-to-bank donation is easier to prove than a hand-to-hand donation. The bank statements show that there has been a transfer and it would be difficult to refute that a transfer has taken place on a certain date.

However, how do you prove that it was not e.g. a loan that has to be reimbursed?

Finally, just like a hand-to-hand donation, the bank transfer in itself cannot contain the terms of the agreement in writing and that makes it difficult to attach any conditions (see p. 144).

### How to donate with a bank transfer?

To give money by way of a donation from one bank account to another, all you need to do is give instructions to the bank to make the transfer. The beneficiary does not even need to have an account with the same bank or in the same country.

Let us take the example of Tom and his son Sonny. Tom plans to make a transfer to Sonny's account and announces that in a registered letter so that he can prove the date of the offer to donate.

We would suggest using A3 paper that you fold it in two and then in three so that the outside half becomes the envelope. Seal with scotch tape on the three open sides. The post office will put the postmark on the stamp on the outside part of the piece of paper and that cannot be separated from the letter. We suggest you send the letter with a return receipt message (*accusé de reception*) which can be signed by Sonny upon receipt and returned to Tom.

When he has received the bank transfer, Sonny thanks his father in a registered letter. The donation is proven with the two registered letters, the bank statements showing the money is going off Tom's account and arriving on Sonny's bank account.

Sonny must keep the two original letters, a copy of the statements showing that the money has left John's account and has arrived on his own account. A model of these letters can be found in the annexes.

## A private agreement

Tom and Sonny may want to draw up separate agreement (called *pacte adjoint*) confirming that Tom has made a donation and that Sonny has accepted the donation. That is a private agreement that must not be registered, and that means that gift tax is not due. However, if and when necessary, this agreement can be registered.

Attaching conditions to a hand-to-hand or a bank-to-bank donation is not simple. It is easier to agree terms and conditions in an agreement signed simultaneously by the donor and the beneficiary, rather than listing these in a letter signed by the donor and in an acceptance letter signed by the beneficiary after the donation.

In that private agreement Sonny can agree that he will use the money to buy a property, that when he marries, the donation will not become community property, that he will not pass the donation on to his spouse, partner or to anyone else, and that if Sonny dies before his father, the donation will revert to Tom. We will go into more detail about these conditions on p. 144. A model can be found in the annexes.

However, a private agreement can get lost or be contested if it is not drawn up in a notarial deed as the law prescribes. Also, a well-drawn up notarial deed is enforceable; you do not need to go to court to enforce it.

## Dutch or Swiss notary

An alternative is to pass the donation before a foreign notary who will not charge Belgian gift tax. However, notaries in most countries tend to charge local tax even if the deed is a donation between foreigners to the country. The only real options are Dutch or Swiss notaries who only charge gift tax if the donor or the beneficiary is a local.

A donation before a Dutch or a Swiss notary is equally valid as a donation before a Belgian notary, but without the gift tax. The terms and conditions cannot be disputed by anyone and, in particular, the date of the notarial deed gives absolute proof of the date that cannot be contested by the tax authorities. Moreover, as a notarial deed it is enforceable in itself.

However, even after a donation before a Dutch or a Swiss notary, the donor must live for another three years, just like with a hand-to-hand donation. As long as the donor lives for another three years, the donation will not be added to her estate when the inheritance tax is calculated. In an emergency situation, a copy of the (Dutch or Swiss) notarial deed can be presented for registration to the tax office and 3% gift tax will be due on the value of the donation at the time of registration.

# And if the worst happens ... some backup solutions

If you avoid gift tax with a hand-to-hand donation, with a bank transfer or a donation before a foreign notary, the equation is "0% gift tax and three years = 3% gift tax and 0 years", meaning that if you pay 3% gift tax, you do not need to outlive the donation by any period of time.

These three years are, therefore a risk. If the donor dies within three years following a tax exempt donation, inheritance tax will become due at rates between 3 and 65 or 80%.

If a donation is made by a couple, e.g. the parents to their children, it may be useful to split the donations and to make sure that each parent gives separately. If one parent dies within three years the inheritance tax will only be due on half of the donations. If one parent becomes ill, the donation documents can still be registered and gift tax paid to avoid inheritance tax will be due. However, gift tax will only be due on one donation.

### Insure the risk

It is always possible to take out insurance to cover the risk of an untimely death of the donor. If the donor dies within the three years, the insurance company will pay a capital that will cover the inheritance tax. It is advisable that the beneficiary pays the premium; if the donor pays the premium, the insured capital paid out by the insurance company would need to be declared in his inheritance tax return.

### Emergency measures

If the donor falls ill within that time frame of three years after the exempt donation, the beneficiary can register the donation by presenting the documents (the exchange of registered mails and the private agreement or the deeds of the donation before a Dutch notary) to the registration tax collector. You do not need to do this in front of a notary.

To simplify the registration, it is useful to mention in which of the three regions the donor has been living in the last five years before the registration. A certificate from the commune may be useful. That will help determine in which region the donor is deemed to have lived during the last five years, and in which region the gift tax is due.

The gift tax will be due at the rate for donations of movables. It will be calculated on the value of the assets on the date of the registration, not at the time of the donation. If the value of the assets has dropped since the donation, then the new value will be used. It is advisable to bring a banker's draft for the registration tax due. That is as good as cash so that you can ask the taxman to register the documents immediately rather than to wait until he has the money on his account.

If timing is of the essence, e.g. because the bank to bank donation happens the day before the donor's death, it may be advisable to register the donation on the day of the donation. However, the registration tax office is only open to the public between 8 and 12 on working days only.

Fortunately, you can take the documents to any registration tax office, it must not be that of your or the donor's residence. If you want to register on the day of the death, you will have to prove the exact time of the death. It may be preferable to pass via a notary.

### Leave Belgium

A final solution may be to leave Belgium for another country that has no inheritance tax or that will not look in your past to see if you have made any donations in the past that has to be included in your estate.

# ATTACH CONDITIONS TO YOUR GIFT

Donations are mostly inspired by tax reasons, but donors do not like to give their bonds and shares away completely. They like to keep the income and they like to keep control over what the beneficiary does with the donation.

What are the most common concerns of donors?

## Keep the income

Most donors need the income from the assets they want to give away. The problem is that you cannot give your cake away and eat it later. In Belgium "*donner et retenir ne vaut*".

Parents can give real property, the family home or another property, to the children and keep the usufruct. That means that they continue to live in the family home or let it out and collect the rent. The gift tax will be due on the full value of the property, but the rates can be kept low by spreading the donation over time.

A portfolio of shares can be donated with the donor retaining the usufruct, and that is possible at reduced gift tax rates for movables (3 and 7%, but 3.3, 5.5 and 7.7% in Wallonia).

That can be done in a notarised donation, but it can also work with a bank donation. The bank opens an account on which the shares and bonds are blocked in the name of the bare owners, usually the children. The income the dividends and interest, will be paid in another account for the parents who have retained usufruct.

Because such usufruct constructions are liable to inheritance tax, one cannot rely on the three year rule to avoid gift tax. Unless gift tax has been paid, inheritance tax is due.

One solution is to pass before a notary, the other is to draw up a private agreement signed by the donor and the beneficiary confirming that this bank transfer constitutes an indirect donation. This statement is then registered with the Ministry of Finance and the lower gift tax rates will be payable. Because gift tax has been paid, inheritance tax is not due. That is not an option if you live in Wallonia because gift tax is not due in that situation.

An alternative is to make the donation subject to an obligation for the beneficiary to pay the donor a fixed amount every month or every year, upon request, if so requested. The reason is to give the parents the income or some means of pressure if they unexpectedly need some income.

## Keep control over the assets

Protect the beneficiary against himself

Most parents want to protect their children against themselves. If they get money too young, they may want to spend it rather than work. Moreover, they may find a taste for illicit substances and spend it all.

The donation may be made subject to the condition that the stocks or property donated shall not be sold, or shall be monitored by a guardian who must look after the interests of the children. The donor could also impose a condition subsequent that if they misbehave, the donation can be revoked by the donor. Such conditions must be carefully drafted.

### The beneficiary dies before the donor

It happens that a child dies before his parent. That can lead to some strange unwanted consequences, e.g. when a son had received a donation from his parents. If the son dies unmarried and with no children, then the parents will inherit the money they had given to their son and pay inheritance tax.

It is always advisable to provide for a contractual reversion so that if the child dies before his/her parents, the donation is annulled. This is called *beding van conventionele terugkeer / clause de retour conventionnel*). The money goes back to the parents and no inheritance tax is due.

### Protect the beneficiary against her spouse

Some donors fear that their handsome son-in-law is only out after their money, and that he will spend it before abandoning their daughter.

Including a condition that the donation may never become community property can be a solution. If their daughter dies before giving birth, the assets donated will return to her own family rather than go to her in-laws.

### Give an heir more than the others

When a donor makes a gift to one of his heirs, it will be assumed that he wanted to give him or her and advance on his inheritance. He can confirm that by mentioning that clearly *"als voorschot op erfenis" / "en advancement d'hoirie"*.

However, if he wants to give him more than the others, he must clearly stat the that the donation is made in advance over and above his equal share with the other heirs (*bij vooruitmaking en buiten erfdeel / par préciput et hors part)*.

# CLEVER DONATIONS

There are a number of tax efficient techniques that have been developed over the years to minimise gift and inheritance tax. These may be seen as aggressive tax planning by the tax authorities and require careful planning with professional advice.

## A reciprocal donation

This technique works as follows. The husband donates his separate property (e.g. stocks worth €300,000) to his wife and his wife reciprocates with a donation of her separate property (e.g. bonds and savings worth €250,000) to her husband. However, each donation is made under the condition that if the beneficiary dies before the donor, the donation is rescinded. If the husband dies first, his wife recovers the bonds and savings worth €250,000 through a contractual reversion so that she has all the family assets worth €550,000.

If the donation was made more than three years before the husband dies, no gift tax is due and the inheritance tax can be validly avoided. However, it is advisable to make the donation before a notary and pay gift tax. The Ruling Committee has accepted that gift tax is only due on the donation with the highest value if the donations are linked. In this case this s on €300,000.

There are a few considerations to be taken into account.

While donations can only be revoked in specific circumstances (ingratitude, attempted murder on the donor, etc...) donations between husband and wife are always revocable, which may reassure husband and wife.

A reciprocal donation cannot be used to circumvent the forced heirship rules. The children may claim that they have been disinherited in order to rescind the donation.

Finally, a reciprocal donation is not possible with community property. Husband and wife own community property together and cannot receive what they already own. If the couple changes its matrimonial property regime to convert community property into separate property, before making a reciprocal donation, the tax authorities have already announced that they will consider to be tax abuse.

# A joint donation by both spouses

If spouses do not have a matrimonial regime of community property, one parent may own all the family assets. If he makes a donation of real property, the gift tax rate is progressive and will be calculated on all the assets at the higher rates. A saving of the gift tax rates could be achieved if the donation was made by both spouses, the lower tax rates would apply twice.

A simple tax planning technique would be for the parents to transmute their separate properties into community property (without gift tax) and to do a donation together.

For real property, this would mean that the transfer is calculated at the lower gift tax rates twice.

For movables, this should not make much difference as the gift tax rate is fixed, but it might have an effect on the inheritance tax rate if the donation is to be included in the inheritance because it occurred less than three years before.

The tax authorities are likely to consider that as aggressive tax planning.

# Donation-division

When parents have a property that they want to give to their son rather than to their two daughters, they could consider selling the property but that attracts purchase tax at 12.5% (10% in Flanders). The alternative is to make a donation to their son but his sisters could later claim that their brother has received much more that they inherit ("look at the value of the house now").

A lifetime gift followed by a buy-out (*dubbele akte / double acte* or *schenking-verdeling / donation-partage*) can solve that problem. The parents donate the property, before a notary, to their three children together, as an advance on their inheritance. Immediately afterwards, in a separate notarial deed, the son buys out his sisters for the agreed price. This will prevent discussions amongst the children later; they have agreed to sell them their share for a fair price.

Moreover, this technique will normally be cheaper than the purchase tax of 12.5%; the gift tax rates on real property (to three children) are lower and the sales tax between co-owners is 1% (2.5% in Flanders).

This is also a proper alternative for the inter vivos distribution by the parents (see p. 176).

# A pass through donation

An alternative way of controlling your estate is a pass through donation. This is similar to the pass through bequest. It allows you to decide twice who receives your donation. In the donation you appoint the second beneficiary who will receive the donation upon the death of the first beneficiary of the donation. We refer to what we said about the pass through bequest above, about the possible uses and the pitfalls.

Not all pass through bequests are allowed. If you want the first beneficiary to keep the donation intact, he must be your son or daughter or your brother or sister and the second beneficiary must be their child or children. If the first beneficiary can use the donation, and only has to pass on what is left over after his death, you can appoint anyone as your beneficiaries.

A pass through donation is deemed to be a double donation and gift tax will be due twice. The gift tax will be due on each transfer, on the value at the time of that transfer. However, the rate of the second transfer will be the rate that applied at the time of the first transfer for a donation or bequest from the original donor to the second beneficiary.

*E.g.   If a grandfather living in Brussels, donates the shares of his company worth €1,000,000 to his son with the obligation for his son to pass them on to his grandson upon the death of the son, gift tax will be due at 3%, that is €30,000. When the son dies, the grandson receives the shares. He does not pay inheritance tax but gift tax at 3% as if he had received a donation from his grandfather. If the shares are then worth €2,000,000, that will be only €60,000; inheritance tax would have been €535,750.*

# Using debt to pay less inheritance tax

If you have real property you can only donate that at the higher gift tax rates. Alternatively, you can spread that over a period of time. However, you will never be able to match the low gift tax rates for movables. Some banks may propose that you take out a loan against your property and donate the cash.

That may help save on inheritance tax as well. If your only heirs are your nieces and nephews and your most important asset is a valuable house, your nieces and nephews risk paying inheritance tax at the highest rates.

What the bank will propose is that you take out a loan to donate cash to your family and that they use the cash to invest, preferably with the bank. When you die, your nieces and nephews pay back the loan with this investment. Little inheritance tax will be due because the loan will be set off against the value of your house.

## Write an I.O.U.

Of course, you cannot just write an I.O.U. and give that to someone to reduce the inheritance tax on your estate. The tax authorities do not look favourably on such actions.

A debt that is only acknowledged in your will is not a debt but a bequest and inheritance tax will be due. That rule has been extended to disguised donations on which no gift tax has been paid. What you are doing is recognizing in a notarial deed that you owe money or one of your prized possessions to the beneficiary who is present to accept. The gift tax rate on movables is a low fixed rate.

This can only work if you have the money or the possession and are effectively in a position to give it. You agree to make the donation but the actual handover will only take place later.

This may be seen as aggressive tax planning but there may be good reasons for it; it helps you control your assets until your death. However, it does not sit well with the principle "*donner et retenir ne vaut*" and the taxman may take the position that you have never had the intention to give. Moreover, the debt may not be allowed as a deduction from your estate so that inheritance tax may be due.

## Gifts that take effect upon the death of the donor

A donation of movables can be made before a Belgian notary at the lower gift tax rates. It would be tempting to make a donation and say "I give you this today, but you only get it on the day I die".

In Brussels and in Flanders such a donation subject to the condition precedent of the donor's death is liable to inheritance tax. In Wallonia, such donation is liable to gift tax at the same rates as real property.

# CHANGE YOUR MARRIAGE CONTRACT

The matrimonial property regime you have may have an effect on what happens to your estate when you die. We have explained the concept of matrimonial property regime above in the chapter on community property.

In case of death, the marriage contract comes first. The marital property regime must be settled before the heirs can have any claims.

If husband and wife have community property, the community property must be distributed upon death and the surviving spouse is entitled to half of the community property. The other half goes into the estate of the deceased that is inherited – and possibly divided – between the heirs, including the surviving spouse, who inherits usufruct on the estate of the deceased.

If husband and wife have separation of properties, there is nothing to divide up. Each spouse owns his own property separately. The property of the deceased is inherited by the heirs and the surviving spouse in accordance with the inheritance rules.

Part of the estate planning can be changing your marriage contract so that you ensure your spouse gets more out of the family assets. If you have community property, you can agree on a distribution that is not 50/50. If you have separate properties, you can agree that, at the end of the marriage, you will pretend you had community property.

## ADVANTAGES

The first advantage of planning your estate with a marriage contract is that it is a durable solution. A donation between husband and wife can always be revoked just like a will. A marriage contract cannot be changed without the consent of your spouse. Depending on how you look at it, that may be a disadvantage as well.

Changing a marriage contract gives immediate tax optimisation. You do not have to wait three years before the tax planning becomes effective.

Finally, a marriage contract is not a donation nor a bequest. It is a contractual arrangement between husband and wife where they agree to keep and own everything they earn or acquire during their marriage in community property or in separate properties.

The forced heirship rules restrict their freedom to give their possessions away through a lifetime gift or in their will but it does not restrict their freedom to make contracts. If they infringe these rules, bequests and donations can be reduced; marriage contracts cannot.

However, sometimes a change of marriage contract can be considered to be a disguised donation to get around the forced heirship rules.

## OPTIMIZE YOUR MARRIAGE CONTRACT

### Go for separation of properties

There are many reasons to exclude community property during one's professional career and keep separate properties in order to protect one's spouse against bankruptcy or against creditors. Another reason may be to keep the assets in the family of one spouse.

When there is no community property, and one spouse is the homemaker, the other builds up – and owns – all the family assets in separate property. That can put the homemaker at a disadvantage. Amongst themselves, husband and wife may consider that they own everything together and they may want to make sure that the contract reflects that.

One solution is to convert the family assets into community property when the reasons to exclude community property have disappeared at the end of one's professional career.

### Separate property with a participation clause

This is a complicated way of saying: "during the marriage we will have separate property, but at the end of the marriage, we will do *as if* we had community property". This is also called "differed community of property".

During your marriage you own the family assets separately but when the marriage ends, through divorce or death of a spouse, the net growth of value of each assets is added up as if it was community property and that is split in two. The spouse whose property has made the biggest gain will have to pay half of the difference to the other.

*E.g.* *if Luis started with €10,000 and his estate is worth 500,000, the accrual is €490,000. If Antonia started with nothing and her estate is worth €750,000 now (through savings and an inheritance from her mother), the accrual is 750,000. Luis has a claim for compensation by Antonia for €750,000 – 490,000 = 260,000 / 2 = €130,000. The end result is that Luis ends up with €630,000, while Antonia only has €620,000. This may seem unfair but both estates have gained €130,000.*

The transfer of €130,000 from Antonia to Luis, if she dies first (or vice versa) is not a donation and, is, therefore, not liable to inheritance tax. However, if a spouse has children from a previous relationship, he cannot give more than the disposable part of his estate to his spouse through such a clause in the marriage contract. The children can get the transfer to the spouse reduced to the disposable share of his estate.

### Make the participation clause optional

If the marriage contract has a participation clause, it may be useful to make it optional. This gives the surviving spouse the option not to exercise his or her claim against the other's estate.

*E.g.* *If Luis had been the only one accruing his estate with e.g. €1,000,000, Antonia can receive €500,000 tax free. However, when she dies, their son will inherit and pay full inheritance tax. Antonia may have been satisfied with an usufruct on the €1,000,000 in Luis' estate and that may save some inheritance tax.*

Making the participation clause optional can be useful for future planning.

## Separate property with community property

Another way of combining the benefits of community property and those of separation of properties is to attach what is called a *"société limitée"*, a limited form of community property for some assets, e.g. for the family home. All other assets remain separate property, but the family home is community property. A preferential distribution provision can be added.

This may be useful for the family home in Flanders on which spouses do not pay inheritance tax.

# Go for community property

In a couple that has opted for separation of properties, one spouse can own all the family assets, e.g. if the other is the homemaker. When the first spouse dies, the children inherit these assets with an usufruct for the homemaker; we have explained the drawbacks of usufruct above.

Most couples in Belgium have the default matrimonial property regime, i.e. community property for everything they earned or acquired after their marriage. Everything they owned before or receive or inherit during the marriage is separate property. If one spouse comes from a rich family, that separate property may be sizeable. If there are no children, the spouse only inherits an usufruct on that property. Upon his death, the assets go to the in-laws.

Opting for full community property may be a way of solving the problem of separate properties and leaving more to one's spouse. Upon the death of one spouse, the surviving spouse already owns half of the community property, and that is before the inheritance rules apply. As an heir she inherits the other half in usufruct while the children inherit the bare ownership. If there are no children, the family assets are community property, the surviving spouse has half of the community property and she inherits her husband's half of the community property. Nothing goes back to the in-laws.

Transforming separate property into community property may be a way of donating half of the separate property to one's spouse. If they change their marriage contract to go for community property and they contribute equal amounts, there is no problem.

If, however, the wife puts more assets in community property, and the husband survives and gets all the community property, then half of the contribution of his wife is a donation that can be reduced in favour of the reserved heirs.

*E.g. Kurt and Jacqueline got married with a contract of community property. Jacqueline had an apartment worth €600,000 that she put into community property, while Kurt only brought €100,000 in savings. When Jacqueline dies ten years later, the community property is given to Kurt, but anything in excess of half of Jacqueline's contribution is a donation.*

## Preferential distribution of community property

When a couple has community property and the marriage ends, the community property must be distributed and each spouse is entitled to half. Modulating the distribution rules helps to care for the surviving spouse. This sort of provision can, of course, only work if there is community property; couples with separate properties must find alternatives.

*E.g. Brendan and Siobhán had been married for 29 years when Brendan developed cancer. Their notary advised them to draw up a marriage contract. Since they were Irish and married before 2004, they did not have community property. Brendan had been the breadwinner and everything he earned was his; Siobhán would only receive the usufruct of his separate property. Upon her death these assets would then go to his nieces and nephews who inherited the bare ownership from their uncle Brendan.*

With this sort of provision, the couple can even disinherit the children they had together. They cannot use this to disinherit children from a previous relationship, if this clause in the marriage contract gives the surviving spouse more than the disposable part of his estate to the estate of the deceased. The children can get the transfer to his spouse reduced to the disposable share of his estate.

### The survivor will have first choice

A first option is to allow the survivor to take certain goods that are common property. This is called a *vooruitmakingsbeding / clause de préciput,* it allows the surviving spouse to have the first pick of what is in the estate of the deceased and that will not be deducted from his/her share of the community property. This can be useful to make sure the surviving spouse received properties that are emotionally important for him/her.

### The survivor gets everything

Another first option is to add a provision to the marriage contract to the effect that all the community property goes to the surviving spouse. This attribution clause is called *verblijvingsbeding / clause d'attribution de communauté* or colloquially *langst leeft al / au dernier vivant tous les biens*. In other words "the survivor gets all the community property".

> *By drawing up a marriage contract, Brendan and Siobhán can convert all the family assets in community property. And by adding an attribution clause, Siobhán will also receive his half of the community property (the other half is hers anyway). There is nothing Brendan's nieces and nephews can do about it; they are not forced heirs.*

Since the marriage contract is a contract, the forced heirship rules cannot stop a couple from giving the community property to the surviving spouse and disinheriting all the children upon the death of the first parent. They cannot invoke the forced heirship rules. However, children from a previous marriage can claim that they are robbed of their reserved share in their parent's inheritance.

This provision is not tax efficient though. The surviving spouse pays inheritance tax on half of the community property, but when her children inherit from her, they will pay inheritance tax on those assets again. However, since husband and wife do not pay inheritance tax on the family home (in Flanders only), it may be useful to include this provision for the family home alone.

There are three variations of the attribution clause that can be used to reduce the inheritance tax and to counter any claims from the children from a previous marriage.

### Attribution clause with multiple choice

A first variation is an attribution allowing the surviving spouse to choose out of a list of options. That gives the surviving spouse the opportunity to see what the best option is at that moment in time, in the light of the relations with the children and of inheritance tax due.

The most common options are: all the community property; half the community property (in full ownership) and the other half in usufruct; usufruct of the community property;      the real property included in the community property; the movable assets (furniture, securities, cash, the car, art, ...) in the community property; usufruct of the real property and full ownership of the movables; full ownership of the family home and usufruct of the rest of the community property; etc.

The marriage contract can determine how the surviving spouse has to make the choice (in a notarial deed or in the inheritance tax return) and in what timeframe (e.g. four months, since the inheritance tax return must be filed within four months). It can also provide what happens if the surviving spouse does not make a choice, e.g. she gets the full community property.

### Attribution clause with compensation

A second variation is an attribution clause that gives the surviving spouse the community property but with an obligation to pay a price to the deceased's heirs. It is advisable to let the surviving spouse choose the assets he/she wants from the community property. This choice will be binding for the heirs. If the value of the chose assets is more than half the value of the community property, the surviving spouse will have to pay compensation for the difference.

The marriage contract will set out how the compensation will be paid, and when (at any time, in several payments or at the time of the surviving spouse). To preserve the inheritance of the other heirs, the compensation can be index linked or bear interest at a rate to be determined.

Moreover, it may be advisable to provide that the heirs may be able to oblige the surviving spouse to pay the price immediately, e.g. if he/she remarries or is declared incompetent to manage his/her own affairs, etc ...

For inheritance tax purposes, the price to be paid can be deducted from the surviving spouse's inheritance, but it would be added to the inheritance of the heirs. However, as it is only due upon the second death, only the net present value can be deducted. The tax authorities are, however, taking the view that they expect the surviving spouse to declare the value of an usufruct on the compensation.

Moreover, if the compensation has not been paid at the time of the death of the second spouse, it is a debt that can be set off against the value of her estate.

### A deathbed provision in a marriage contract

Belgian tax lawyers can be inventive in their tax planning. They found a flaw in the law that they used to work out a form of last minute estate planning that they called the "deathbed construction" (*sterfhuisconstructie / construction de la mortuaire*).

E.g.  *In the example above, when Brendan dies, the community property becomes Siobhán's property and she has to pay inheritance tax on Brendan's half.*

*However, the notary pointed out that a small change to the marriage contract could save her a lot of inheritance tax. If they wrote in the marriage contract that at the end of the marriage, be it through divorce or death, "Siobhán receives everything" rather than "the surviving spouse receives everything", no inheritance tax is due.*

That is due to a quirk in the inheritance tax code. What you receive from the marriage contract is not strictly speaking an inheritance. That is why the inheritance tax code had to assimilate this attribution to a bequest. Inheritance tax is due on whatever one receives from the community property in excess of one's own half of the community property. That provision is written "subject to the condition of surviving one's spouse". If, however, the marriage contract states that one spouse, e.g. Siobhán, receives everything in any event, whether she survives the other or not, no inheritance tax will be due.

There has been some litigation about this provision that was definitively settled in favour of the tax payer by the Supreme Court in 2010. The tax authorities are now calling this aggressive or abusive tax planning.

# Other Reasons for a Marriage Contract

## Reassure your children

After Howard lost his second wife, it took him a long time to get over the loss of Suzanne, they had been married for thirty years. His sons, Pierre and Jean-Charles, wanted to see him settled, and they were happy to hear he met someone special. Their delight turned to shock when they met Nicole. After all, at 26, she was 63 years younger than their father.

And then Pierre and Jean-Charles started thinking: "Of course, dad could not disinherit us entirely, we are each entitled to a third, but if Nicole receives an *usufruct*, she sits on their inheritance for the rest of her life, and that can be a long time. She might even want to claim usufruct on the shares and bonds he had given them a year ago retaining the usufruct for himself.

Nicole realised that all Pierre and Jean-Charles were worried about was their rights to their father's inheritance, and she did not even want a piece of that. All she wanted was some happiness with Howard.

Senator Valckeniers faced the same problem and discovered he could not make an agreement with his new wife to make her abandon her entitlement to the usufruct on his estate. He introduced a bill and got the law changed in 2003. A married couple can now waive any inheritance rights to each other's estate but only to protect children from a first marriage or a previous relationship. If neither has children, they cannot do that, not even to protect nieces and nephews.

The solution for Nicole and Howard is to draw up a marriage contract of full separation of property, thereby excluding all community property, and to include a provision to the effect that they waive any claims to each other's inheritance. A unilateral waiver by Nicole would do as well. In fact, they are disinheriting each other. However, Nicole can never waive her right to usufruct on Howard's house if that is the family home.

This solution is not limited to Belgians but it is set up for the situation where they die in Belgium. If they move abroad, this waiver will only have effect if the local law permits it. It can even be used to change an existing marriage contract; it does not have to be signed before the marriage.

In fact, what Pierre and Jean-Charles do not realise is that Nicole and Howard can always change their marriage contract and drop that provision in their marriage contract. Moreover, it does not stop Howard from making donations to Nicole. If she has waived her inheritance rights, she definitively loses the right to usufruct on the shares and bonds on which Howard had given the bare ownership to his children.

## REGISTERED PARTNERS?

Registered partners cannot sign a marriage contract, tontine or an accruer clause can help (see p. 176).

# PLANNING WITH AN INSURANCE POLICY

Life insurance is an important part in any estate plan. It can give your heirs the cash to pay off your debts or taxes or the inheritance tax that will be due on your estate. It can secure funds to ensure a financial future for your spouse or partner, or a schooling fund for your children. It can also be a way to ensure the survival of a business or partnership.

However, life insurance has also become a normal part of every investment strategy: life insurance as a way of saving for our old age and then hopefully leaving an inheritance for the children.

## LIFE INSURANCE: THE TECHNIQUE

Life insurance is a contract with an insurance company that undertakes to pay an amount of money to the policyholder or to the beneficiary appointed by the policyholder, either upon the death of the insured, or at the agreed end date if the insured is still alive, as determined in the policy.

## A contract with three parties

Apart from the insurance company, there are three parties to any life insurance policy.

### The policyholder

The policyholder takes out insurance and pays the premium. He takes out life insurance on the life of a person, the insured. He also decides who will be the *beneficiary* who will receive the insured capital.

Until the insured dies, the controls the policy. He has the right to appoint or change the beneficiaries. He can redeem the policy or reduce the insured capital and take back some of this savings. The policyholder can also ask for an advance on the policy, put a pledge or a lien on the policy, or transfer the rights under the insurance policy.

There is one exception; when the policyholder allows the beneficiary to accept the benefit of the policy (in an endorsement (*bijvoegsel / avenant*) to the policy signed by the policyholder, the insurance company and the beneficiary, he will need the beneficiary's written agreement. in writing.

### The insured

Strictly speaking, the insured has no say in the policy. He is just the risk insured. If you take out insurance on your wife's life and appoint yourself as the beneficiary, that is something that is completely outside her control.

The insurance policy can be taken out on several lives. A joint life insurance insures two or more lives with the proceeds payable on the first death (*joint life first death*) or second death (*joint life second death*).

A policy can be taken out by several policyholders, e.g. when the family savings are used to pay the premium. When one policyholder dies, the other policyholder exercises the rights of the policyholder on his own.

### The beneficiary

The beneficiary is the person who has been designated to receive the insured benefit. The policyholder can appoint primary and secondary beneficiaries; the latter receive the insured capital if the primary beneficiaries have died before the insured.

If no beneficiary has been appointed, the insurance company will pay the benefit to the estate of the policyholder, that is to his heirs.

With mixed life insurance, there can be a different beneficiary for the living benefits (during the life of the beneficiary - usually the policyholder himself) and a beneficiary for the death benefits (upon the insured's death.

The policyholder, the insured and the beneficiary can be three people:

E.g.  *Elias takes out life insurance on Janine's life for the benefit of their son, Teddy. However, the same person can just as well be policyholder, the insured and the beneficiary, depending on what he wants to achieve. If Elias wants to save for himself, he takes out insurance on his own life and for his own benefit.*

# Branch 21 and Branch 23

In Belgium, popular policies for saving and investing are called Branch 21 and Branch 23 insurance policies.

Branch 21 policies offer a guaranteed return on top of the invested capital; they are a tax efficient alternative for investments in bonds. The premium can be monthly, quarterly, half yearly or annual. These are savings that you put away. It can also be a single premium, i.e. an earlier investment that you invest.

Branch 23 insurance policies are unitised life assurance policies linked to one or more investment funds. The premiums are invested in UCITS (Undertakings for Collective Investments in Transferable Securities) funds with various levels of risk. The capital is not guaranteed and neither is the return. They are also called "insurance wrappers": your premium buys you a fund wrapped in an insurance policy. When you buy an insurance wrapper, the premium is the capital you invest

Branch 21 and branch 23 policies are popular because the return within the insurance policy is not taxable as long as certain terms are met.

## Clearing up some misunderstandings

Investing in an insurance policy is a technique that hard to grasp at first. When you take out life insurance, make sure that you work with an insurance broker who is registered with the Financial Services and Markets Authority, the FSMA (www.fsma.be) who will explain how insurance works.

### The surprises of life insurance

While insurance policies have a very favourable income tax regime, a premium tax of 2% is due on the amount of the premiums paid if the policy holder is living in Belgium.

When you invest in an insurance policy, you must never take the projected return for granted or guaranteed. Past returns are an indication and not a guarantee of future returns.

As for Branch 21 policies, the insurance company pays an annual guaranteed return and profit participation, but that is not guaranteed for future premiums. In the 1980s, returns of 6 to 10% were normal;

these rates are not realistic anymore. Even the guaranteed return can be reduced.

The value of Branch 23 policies depends on the underlying funds; they can go up, but they can just as well go down. You can actually lose your investment.

When the insured person dies, the insurance company pays out the insured capital. For Branch 23 policies, it sells the UCITS in the insurance wrapper even if they just happen to underperform and pays out the value proceeds to the beneficiary of the death benefits. He cannot ask to postpone the payment and hold on to the UCITS for a while.

People who have taken out life insurance as an alternative for a savings account are often surprised to hear that the insurance company asks for the original policy before paying out; the policy is proof of ownership.

### Dormant policies

An insurance policy may become dormant because the policyholder has forgotten all about the policy (e.g. a group insurance with a previous employer) or because the beneficiary has never been told about it, or has moved and become untraceable.

Banks and insurance companies have many dormant or unclaimed policies. As yet, they do not have an obligation to search for the beneficiaries. It is the beneficiary who must contact the bank or insurance company and prove that the insured has died. This is just another reason why it is advisable to keep a personal affairs checklist and a binder with copies of the policies (see p. 201).

### The beneficiary is not clearly appointed

Another reason why a life insurance policy may become dormant is that the beneficiary is appointed in terms that are too vague. If the bank or insurance company cannot identify the beneficiary, they have no obligation to go out and find him.

Be careful who you appoint as your beneficiary. If you appoint the beneficiary in general terms like "my husband" or "my children", the insurance company will take that literally, and pay to your husband or your children. When you separate from your husband, he will remain your husband and collect, while you may have wanted your new partner to receive the capital. He will only become your husband when you remarry. If your son dies, your daughter will collect but your son's children may not; they are not your children.

The bank or insurance company are not supposed to be able to read your mind. Avoid any ambiguity; review your policies from time to time and if necessary, use names and addresses instead. However, it may still be advisable to keep the appointment of the beneficiaries general: the spouse, the children, the grandchildren. When you remarry, when you have children with your second wife, or when you acquire more grandchildren, they are automatically included in the group of beneficiaries. But you may want to review your beneficiaries' clause from time to time.

### The beneficiary dies before the insured

When the beneficiary dies before the insured, his heirs do not automatically become the beneficiaries. If no secondary beneficiary has been appointed, the policy has no beneficiaries, and the insurance company will pay out to the policyholder. When the insured dies, it is the policyholder who collects the insured capital.

If the insured is also the policyholder, the insured capital will be paid out to his estate and distributed amongst his heirs.

# AN ALTERNATIVE TO A WILL?

Life insurance can also be taken out as an alternative to a will in order to pass assets to beneficiaries. When you take out life insurance on your own life, and you appoint your children as beneficiaries, you achieve the same result as when you make a will. You pay a single premium, or you pay regular premiums, and during your lifetime you are the beneficiary. When you die, your children receive the benefit.

When you use life insurance as an alternative for a will, you need to take account of the cost of life insurance: a 2% premium tax, the entry fees and the exit fees.

## Asset protection

When you die, your beneficiary claims the payment directly from the insurance company, not from your heirs. This can be useful to provide funds to someone who would not otherwise inherit from you, e.g. a partner or a stepchild, and who would prefer not to have to ask your heirs. Inheritance tax will be due as if it was a bequest, and the tax rate will be the tax rate for partners and stepchildren.

When you die, your debts do not die with you. Your creditors can enforce their claim on your estate but not on the insured capital; they cannot ask that the insurance company pays them or appoints them as your beneficiaries for the death benefits.

We have explained that upon death the bank blocks the accounts. A final advantage of life insurance is that the insurance company does not have to do that, and that it can pay out the insured capital.

## Life insurance and forced heirship

Life insurance has a special status in the law. It is a contract with an insurance company and, until recently, it could not be attacked with the forced heirship rules.

A life insurance policy could be used to disinherit the children in favour of a mistress or to disinherit the children from a previous marriage or relationship in favour of a new partner or spouse.

The law was changed in 2013; if the life insurance policy is a donation in disguise, it may be added to the estate as if it were a donation. If necessary, the heirs may ask the court that the insured capital be returned to the estate, in part or entirely until their reserved share is guaranteed.

E.g.    *Mr Ash, father of two children, used all his savings (€1,000,000) to subscribe a policy appointing himself as the beneficiary for his living benefits and his partner, Miss Wood, for the death benefits, leaving just some furniture and the bills for his children.*

*The children will have no problem showing that insurance was a donation. The court can oblige Miss Wood to return the insured capital and share it with the children. Since the children have a protected right to two thirds, they will receive two thirds, and Miss Wood will keep a third.*

If the beneficiary of the policy is also one of the heirs, the law assumes that the policyholder has released the beneficiary from the obligation to return the insured capital. If he wants the beneficiary to return the insurance capital to his estate, he must make an express statement to that effect. Otherwise, it will be seen as an advance on the beneficiary's inheritance.

# INHERITANCE TAX

The taxman discovered that life insurance can be a valid alternative for a will. For inheritance tax purposes, it does not make any difference whether you leave something by will or through an insurance policy. Inheritance tax will due.

## Life insurance on your own life

When you take out a policy on your own life, the related death benefits will be liable to inheritance tax as if you had left that money in your will. It is taxed on top of everything else that the beneficiary inherits. That means that the rate of the inheritance tax can go up to 30% if the beneficiary is your child or spouse and up to 80% if he is not a relative at all.

If you have community property and you pay the premium from community property, the death benefit paid to your spouse will be liable to inheritance tax but only for half because, indirectly she paid half the premiums.

## Life insurance on another's life

Inheritance tax is also due on policies taken out on your life by someone else (*e.g.* an employer or your management company) but only when the benefit is paid out at death.

You can, indeed, take out life insurance on someone else's life. The beneficiary will receive the capital when that person dies, and that is a gift from you to the beneficiary that is just delayed until the insured person dies. It is noteworthy that in that case, inheritance tax is only due if it is paid at any time after the death of the policyholder or in the three years before your death.

That may seem strange, but what the taxman is seeing is your money that is blocked in the insurance policy during someone else's life? When that person dies, your money will be paid. Even when you, the policyholder, die the policy just keeps going until the condition materialises.

*Albert wanted to provide for his daughter, Cristiana, and he took out life insurance on her husband's life. Bernhard and Cristiana are still alive and happily married, and the policy has not matured yet.*

*When Bernhard dies in 2038, Cristiana receives €1,000,000, and inheritance tax will be due as if she had received it from her father who died 25 years before. She has to file a new inheritance tax return and pay inheritance tax. That will be calculated at the higher rates because it comes on top of everything she has already inherited from Albert.*

The rule about the three year restriction is similar to the three year rule for hand to hand donations or bank gifts on which no gift tax has been paid. There is, however, a difference. The gift is not made when the policy is signed, but when the benefit is paid out, and it is only if that happens more than three years before the policyholder's death, that no inheritance tax is due.

*If Bernhard had died more than three years before Albert, Cristiana would not have had to include the capital that her father provided for her in his inheritance tax return.*

Albert's son Bob was not that lucky; Albert had taken out a term insurance on the life of his son, Bob. The beneficiary was to be Bob at the age of 18 (if he was still alive – for the living benefits) or Albert himself for the death benefits (that is if Bob had died before he turned 18). Bob did not die and received a capital of €150,000. He had a great party for his 18th birthday on 21 March 2011. However, sSince his father died less than three years later, the €150,000 must be reported in the inheritance tax return. Bob will have to pay inheritance tax on the full amount and he cannot even deduct the cost of the party.

The only time that insurance on another's life does not attract inheritance tax is when you take out life insurance on the life of someone else and appoint yourself as the beneficiary.

*In the example above, if Bob had died before his 18th birthday, Albert would have received the insured capital tax free; it was his money to start with.*

The last example shows one of the ways that you can use insurance to save on inheritance tax. The following exceptions offer possibilities for tax planning.

## What does that mean for estate planning?

If you take out life insurance on your own life, inheritance tax will be due when you die. If you take it out on another's life, inheritance tax will be due when that person dies, even many years after you die.

As long as the policy does not pay out, inheritance is not due, because the conditions are not met. However, the tax authorities are trying to defend the position that they can, nevertheless, charge inheritance tax at the time of the policyholder's death. The tax would then be calculated on the redemption value of the policy. They are assuming that the primary beneficiary will receive the benefit eventually. If, for some reason the primary beneficiary does not receive the benefit (e.g. because he dies before the maturity date), the heirs will have to file a new inheritance tax return to correct the original return.

This position has not been confirmed by the courts.

The only way to avoid inheritance tax is to live three years (and a few days) longer than the person you insured.

## THE BENEFICIARY TAKES OUT INSURANCE

The insured capital is liable to inheritance tax if the insurance is taken out by the policyholder upon his own life. However, no inheritance tax is due if the policyholder has taken out the insurance on someone else's life and appointed himself as the beneficiary. It is a bit like a bet; he has put a premium on another's life and he is just collecting the insured capital.

> When Ben and Bianca take out a life insurance on their life appointing the children as beneficiaries, inheritance is due. However, if the children take out the life insurance on their parents' life but to their own benefit, no inheritance is due.

This principle can be used in the following situations:

# Take out life insurance to pay inheritance tax

We have explained above that no gift tax is due on a hand to hand donation or a bank donation. However, inheritance tax may be due if the donor dies within three years after the donation (see p. 137).

The donor may want to take a temporary insurance that will pay inheritance tax if he were to die before the three years are up. However, when the insurance company pays the inheritance tax due, that capital will be liable to inheritance tax as well.

That is not the case if the beneficiary of the donation takes out insurance on the life of the donor and pays the premium with an additional donation from the donor or if he uses the income from the assets donated to pay the annual premiums.

Whether such insurance is a good idea depends on a few practical considerations. Many insurance companies do not write insurance if the insured is over 65 or 70 and the older the insured the higher the premium. Moreover, the value of the assets may go up or down over the three years; calculating how much inheritance tax will be due can be speculative. Whether such insurance is a good idea depends on whether the premium outweighs the lower gift tax rates on movables.

## Donate the insurance premium

In this scenario, the parents donate their savings to the children on condition that they take out a new life insurance policy on their parents' life. Because the insurance is taken out by the beneficiaries, no inheritance tax will be due.

Parents who want to keep some income from, and control over, their investments can require that the children appoint their parents as beneficiaries for the life benefits or that they give their parents the right to redeem the policy.

That allows the parents to draw money from the insurance policy. An alternative could be that the parents receive an annuity from the return of the insurance policy, but in a financial crisis the policy may not have a sufficient return to pay the annuity.

For that reason, the donation should be made before a notary and gift tax is due at the reduced gift tax rates on movables. We refer to the section on donations and conditions.

## Pay the premium with community property

Community property is owned by both spouses together. If the policyholder pays the premium with community property, he pays half with his own money and half with his wife's money. If his wife is the beneficiary, she has paid half of the premium. Inheritance tax will be due only on the part for which her husband paid the premium.

If husband and wife have separate properties, the entire capital is either taxed or exempt.

If a husband takes out insurance on his own life for the benefit of his wife, he pays the premium with his own money. If he dies first, inheritance tax is due on everything. When she dies before him, the policy does not pay out and no inheritance tax is due. The payment will only come when he dies, and if has not appointed a new beneficiary, it will fall in his estate.

If he takes out insurance on his wife's life for his own benefit, the policyholder is also the beneficiary. When she dies, the policy pays out, and he does not pay inheritance tax. However, if he dies first, the policy continues until his wife dies, and when she dies, the policy will pay out to the husband's estate. His heirs will have to file a new inheritance tax return to correct the original return.

## Cross insurance

This scenario is similar to a reciprocal donation (see p. 146).

If husband and wife have €1,000,000 in family assets, and they do not have community property, they could each take out insurance on the other's life for €500,000.

When your spouse dies, you get back the capital on the insurance you had taken out; no inheritance tax is due. However, the insurance taken out by your spouse on your own life stays blocked in the policy until you die and then it falls in his/her estate and his/her children inherit it. We write blocked because only the policyholder can redeem the policy. When he/she is dead, no one else can do that.

# Pay gift tax to avoid inheritance tax

With donations, you can avoid inheritance tax by paying gift tax.  If you pay gift tax on a donation to your children, they will not have to pay inheritance tax. 3% gift tax can avoid 30% inheritance tax.

The same is true for insurance: no inheritance tax is due if gift tax has been paid.  How can this work?

## Appoint the beneficiary in a donation

Appointing the beneficiary(ies) of an insurance policy in a donation means that the beneficiary accepts the benefit of the insurance policy.

That can be done in a notarial deed, but it must also be included in an endorsement (*bijvoegsel / avenant*) to the policy signed by the policyholder, the insurance company and the beneficiary.

It should be noted that the consequence of the beneficiary accepting the benefit of the policy in an endorsement, is that the policyholder can no longer exercise all his rights anymore. You cannot appoint or revoke the beneficiaries, you cannot redeem the policy, or ask for an advance on the policy if you have the living benefits, or even put a pledge or a lien on the policy or transfer your rights under the insurance policy.  That will only be possible with the written agreement of the beneficiary, if the beneficiary waives the benefit or if he dies before the policy pays out.

if you live in Brussels or Flanders no gift tax would be due when you appoint a beneficiary in your insurance policy. Because the donation is made pending the policyholder's death, only a registration tax of €25 will be due, and that is not enough to avoid the inheritance tax.

If you live in Wallonia, gift tax will be due (at 3.3%, 5.5% or 7.7%) on the value of the insured capital at the time of the registration; the insured capital must not be paid out.  When gift tax is paid, no inheritance tax is due upon death, but only on the amount on which gift tax has been paid.

If the value of the policy goes up and the insurance company pays out a higher capital upon death, the difference (the gain) will be liable to inheritance tax.  That is a likely scenario with Branch 23 investment policies (in the long term). If the insurance company pays out more capital, the difference will be liable to inheritance tax. If, on the contrary, it pays out less, the gift tax cannot be recovered.

There is another risk, if the beneficiary dies before the insured, the gift tax may have been paid in vain. The policyholder is free to redeem the policy.

## Donate the policy

Donating the insurance policy is an alternative, but one that is not regulated by law. For example, if you have taken out a Branch 23 insurance policy, you are the policyholder and normally your life is the life insured. Donating that policy would mean that you transfer the policy as such to e.g. your only son so that he becomes the policyholder of the insurance policy.

If you donate the policy, the policy continues with your son as the policyholder, you as the life insured, and whoever you have appointed as the beneficiary. In principle, gift tax is due at 3% (3.3% in Wallonia) at the time of the donation; it is calculated on the value of the policy at that moment in time. At the time of the insured person's death, the insured capital is paid out and no inheritance tax is due.

## Keep control

There are a few techniques that allow the parents to keep control. E.g. the son appoints one of his parents as a beneficiary for the life benefits or he can give his parent the right to redeem the policy. That allows the parent to draw money from the insurance policy.

However, these may be deemed to be abusive tax planning because you are giving your cake and keeping it to eat it later. Of course, if this secondary planning takes place much later, it is not the parent's decision but the son's to appoint the parent as a beneficiary or to give his parent the right to redeem the policy.

## Joint life insurance

A policy can be taken out by several policyholders. These can be taken out on one life or on both lives, either under the formula *"joint life first death"* or *"'joint life last death"* depending on when the insurance company pays out, that is upon first death or upon second death.

These are usually taken out by a couple with the family savings as the premium under the formula "joint life last death".  Upon the first death, the insurance company does not pay out the capital insured so that the rules that assimilate the life insurance to an inheritance are rendered ineffective at that time. The surviving policyholder can continue to exercise all the policyholder's rights: appoint or revoke the beneficiaries, and even redeem the capital.

It is only upon the second death that Belgian inheritance tax can be due on the insured capital. Half of that has to be declared as part of the estate of the first deceased and half in the estate of the second.

# PLANNING BY CONTRACT

As a matter of principle, you cannot make an agreement with your heirs and spouse about your estate. There is one exception, the inter vivos distribution. There are also a number of contracts that will have an effect on your estate and they can help you plan your estate.

## INTER VIVOS DISTRIBUTION

The *inter vivos* distribution (*ascendentenverdeling / partage d'ascendants*) is an agreement between parents and their children in which the parents distribute their future estate and the children agree. Because the value of properties goes up and down, it may create discussions amongst the children.

Moreover, because it has effect upon their death there is no saving on inheritance tax. The donation-division is a better and safer alternative (see p. 148).

## TONTINE AND ACCRUER CLAUSES

In the 1980s, tontine and accrue clauses were rediscovered as an alternative for a marriage contract between unmarried partners. They could not inherit from each other, and if they appointed each other as a beneficiary in their wills, inheritance tax would have been very high.

Moreover, this bequest was always open to attack by the children from a previous marriage or relationship under the forced heirship rules.

### Tontine

Tontine is a form of life insurance scheme named after the banker Lorenzo de Tonti who invented it in 1653. Investors pay a sum of money and receive annual dividends on their capital. As and when they die, their share in the dividends is reallocated among the surviving investors. The scheme proved a very popular, but members had all interest in making sure they survived. Robert Louis Stevenson describes the excesses to which tontine could lead in his black comedy novel *The Wrong Box*. As a result, tontine was banned in the U.K. and in most states in the U.S.; they fell into disuse in France.

When unmarried partners bought a house together, notaries proposed tontine as a solution. Just like any other couple, they pay the advance together and then take a mortgage together to pay off the purchase price.

By adding a few provisions in the purchase deed, they could create a tontine between them. When one partner dies, the other becomes the owner of the house through tontine rather than through the inheritance law. He does not inherit and he does not receive a donation.

When the surviving partner receives the other's half of the property through tontine, no inheritance tax is due. Nevertheless, property purchase tax will be due at 12.5% (or 10% in Flanders) on this half.

An accruer clause is a variation that can be set up between two partners for assets they already own jointly.

### Tontine and accruer clauses are not a donation

Because both partners put in an equal investment and have an equal chance to survive the other, tontine is not a donation in disguise.

For a tontine to be valid (and tax efficient), both partners must put in an equivalent investment taking account of their chances of survival. That depends on their respective sex, age and health situation. If they are the same age, an equal contribution may seem equivalent, except that women have a higher life expectancy. When they are young, that difference can be overlooked, but what would not stand a chance if there is an equal contribution by two partners with a large age gap.

When their contributions are not equivalent, there is indirectly a donation from the partner who has overpaid and that donation can be attacked by his heirs. If tontine is a donation in disguise, gift tax will be due on the share of the deceased partner. The taxman can assume that the tontine or the accrue clause is in fact a mutual donation and charge gift tax instead of registration tax.

If a tontine or accruer clause is properly set up, the risk of gift tax can be avoided.

Partners should, however, think of all the consequences of tontine. If the surviving partner gains the property, it will go to his heirs when he dies. Is that what they want? If the partner who died first had children from a previous marriage or relationship, they will end up with nothing and they are in fact disinherited.

### Tontine for usufruct

That is why tontine for usufruct alone can be an alternative. The surviving partner then receives the usufruct while he already has the full ownership of his share in the house. This puts the surviving partner and the children of the deceased partner in the same situation as the surviving spouse who inherits usufruct. Upon the death of both partners, the property is owned by the respective families.

The purchase tax on tontine for to usufruct, is the tax due on an usufruct taking into account the age of the surviving partner.

### An investment portfolio in tontine

Tontine is not limited to real property; a couple can hold movables, such as an investment portfolio, bonds, etc.., in tontine. There is no purchase tax when the partners acquire the portfolio, or when a partner dies. This makes it more important to get it right to avoid inheritance tax.

Partners must be careful to make a proper list of the assets held in tontine, and they must write out what happens if the assets are sold, are lost or destroyed. They should be careful to keep all purchase documents and show that they have contributed in accordance with their life expectancy.

### Tontine today

Since registered partners inherit the usufruct of the family home and the furniture in the family home, the need for tontine is much less. Moreover, registered partners and, in Flanders non-registered partners who have lived together for a year, pay the same inheritance tax rates as married couples.

Nevertheless, tontine remains a useful technique for large estates. While the registration tax on the purchase is 12.5% (10% in Flanders) of one and a half times the value of the house, the inheritance tax is still cheaper when the house is worth less than €300,000. For smaller estates, one has to see whether the higher purchase outweighs the other advantages.

A first advantage of tontine is that it cannot be revoked, while a will is always revocable. It offers stronger protection, even between husband and wife. When partners have tontine, both partners must agree to terminate it. That is why tontine is usually set up for short periods of time (two or three years) that are automatically renewed unless either partner gives notice that he does not want to renew.

For the surviving partner, it is often more important that the forced heirs cannot attack the tontine agreement. That is why it is essential to make sure that the contribution of both partners is equivalent and that they have equal chances to become the owner of the house. If that is not the case, the heirs can ask the court to reduce the disguised donation and have their stake in the estate increased.

## SPLIT-PURCHASE SCHEMES

In a split-purchase scheme, the parents buy the usufruct and the children buy the bare ownership of a property. This is tax efficient because usufruct extinguishes upon the parents' death. The children become full owners while they have only paid the purchase tax on the bare ownership rights.

The inheritance tax code considers this as a disguised donation unless the beneficiaries prove the contrary, i.e. that they were in possession of the cash to pay for the bare ownership. This could be through a loan (see below) or following a prior hand to hand donation, a donation before a foreign notary or even a donation before a Belgian notary (with 3% gift tax).

The tax authorities take the position that this is tax abuse, even if the prior donation was registered and gift tax was paid, when there is unity of intent. Such split-purchase scheme (usufruct/bare ownership) would be accepted if you made a donation to your children long before you considered buying the property. In that case, it would be clear that the children have taken the decision to invest in bare ownership of their own volition.

## BANK LOANS

Some banks are promoting personal loans as a means of avoiding inheritance tax. They give you a loan so that you have leverage to build out your wealth. What they imply is that this allows you to donate your assets to your children, while you keep a debt that can be set off against the value of your estate.

If your only heirs are your nieces and nephews and your most important asset is a valuable house, your nieces and nephews risk paying inheritance tax at the highest rates. The bank will suggest that you take out a loan to donate cash to your family; they use the cash to invest (preferably with the bank) and when you die, your nieces and nephews pay back the loan with their investment. No or little inheritance will be due because the loan will be set off against the value of your house.

You can also buy property with your children and take out a bank loan, you buy usufruct and the children bare ownership. Usufruct extinguishes upon your death while the bank loan can be set off against the value of your estate.

An alternative scenario is that you sell the bare ownership of your house to a friend who takes out a bank loan; the purchase tax for real property is 12.5% (10% in Flanders). A few months later, you make a donation for the sales price and the registration tax, so that your friend can reimburse the bank loan. The gift tax will be 7% (7.7% in Wallonia). The total tax will be less than the inheritance tax.

# USING A FAMILY PARTNERSHIP

Rather than giving your investments to your children, you can put them in a family partnership. You can donate your shares in the partnership and keep income and control from your investments for the rest of your life.

## The partnership

A partnership (*burgerlijke maatschap / société civile*) can be set up with a minimum of formalities and at a low cost.

### A partnership is straightforward

The only formal requirement is that all the founding partners sign a simple agreement setting out the articles of association of the partnership. It can be drawn up by a notary, but that is not necessary.

The partnership does not need a minimum share capital, it does not pay company income tax, it does not have to keep accounts or file annual accounts. The partnership is also very discreet: the incorporation or the appointment of directors must not be published in the Belgian Official Journal.

### A partnership is transparent for tax reasons

Because the partnership is not an incorporated legal entity, it is transparent for tax purposes.

There is no transfer tax when assets are put into the partnership, and the income is taxed as if the partners received their share in the income directly.

Real property can be held in a partnership, but that is not advisable. The transfer must be made before a notary and registration tax will be at the rate of 12.5% (10% in Flanders). The donation of shares in a partnership that holds real property would attract gift tax, because the transfer of the real property must be done in a notarised deed. The rates would be the rates of gift tax for real property.

# The family partnership

The partnership is often used for tax and estate planning between parents and children when the parents want to make a donation to all their children.

The parents set up a partnership and transfer their money, securities and art work to the partnership in exchange for shares in the partnership. They get a number of shares that is proportional to the value of the assets they transfer individually.

The parents then give a large part (*e.g.* 98%) of their shares to their children. These shares are movable assets, so that they can be given at the low gift tax rates if the donation is made before a Belgian notary. A donation before a notary allows them to retain the usufruct of the shares and the income, dividends or interest. A donation with retention of usufruct is a bit difficult with a hand to hand donation (see p. 138).

Alternatively, the parents can make the donation subject to an obligation for the children to pay the income or an annuity from the assets to their parents. Since the parents are the directors of the partnership, they can enforce that obligation.

## Administration means control

In the articles of association the parents are appointed as directors for life, and when one parent dies, the other continues as the sole director. As long as they hold some shares, they cannot be removed as administrators even if the children have the majority of the shares.

As directors, the parents control the assets in the partnership. They can sell the assets and reinvest them without the agreement of the children. They could, however, be held liable for the performance of their office.

By imposing strict entry and exit rules in the articles (*e.g.* "with the directors' approval"), they can control who joins the partnership. In particular, this must prevent the children from cashing in by selling their shares in the partnership.

## Income

The partnership is transparent; each partner or shareholder has a share in the income in proportion to the number of shares he holds. If the parents have 2% of the shares and the children 98%, the parents are deemed to receive (and pay tax on) 2% of the income.

However, the articles of association can introduce a rule that the directors will receive a higher share of the income. Alternatively, the parents can keep the usufruct on the shares they have given or an entitlement to receive the income or an annuity from the assets.

That the partnership is transparent means that income tax is calculated as if the partners received their share of the income directly. When the bank pays the interest or dividends, it will calculate the withholding tax due as if it paid the income directly to the partners. That is 25% and usually that is the final tax for the partners.

They do not have to declare the income anymore. Some types of income are tax exempt; *e.g.* if the partnership makes a capital gain on its investment. Capital gains made in the normal management of a private estate are not taxable.

If you have children living abroad, the bank will have to take account of their tax residence to determine whether tax must be withheld. Moreover, these children will probably have to declare the income or capital gains in their tax return abroad.

### When do you donate?

In the example above the parents set up the partnership, transfer their investments into the partnership and give their shares in the partnership to their children. This donation is preferably done before a notary.

An alternative is for the parents to donate their investments to their children subject to the condition that the children then put these assets in a partnership with their parents. The parents put some cash in the partnership so that they hold one or two per cent of the shares. They are appointed as directors as well.

Another alternative possibility is that the parents keep their shares, but in the articles of association there is an accruer clause so that when one of the partners dies, be it a parent or a child, his share accrues to the other partners .

### Winding up the partnership

The partnership is usually set up for the lifetime of its directors. When they die, it is then wound up automatically. The assets revert to the remaining partners who can then distribute the assets.

The partnership can also be set up for an indefinite duration. In that case, the partnership continues after the parents' death. It can be wound up at any time if one of the partners so requests. This may be useful to keep the assets undivided between the children. The articles of association may provide that the partnership is continued between the remaining partners and the heirs of the deceased partners (normally they are the same).

The articles can also provide that the share of a deceased partner accrues to the other partners. Usually, that could be from the parents to the children, but it could also be between the children. When one of the children dies before his parents, his share is not inherited by the parents (with inheritance tax) but it is shared between the other children. This may also be a manner to keep the assets away from the deceased child's spouse or children.

Winding up the partnership does not trigger any tax unless the partnership holds real property.

Moreover, since the parents had donated the shares during their lifetime, no further inheritance tax will be due, except on the shares the parents held. However, if any of the children live in a country where the beneficiaries pay gift or inheritance tax, tax may be due there.

# TRUSTS AND FOUNDATIONS

Trusts are a typical common law answer to many of life's problems in common law countries. Although they are perceived as complicated and expensive things, in reality, they are simply vehicles in which to hold assets for beneficiaries and from which to distribute income, if any has been generated.

The alternative in civil law countries, is the foundation.

## TRUST

Trusts are set up for convenience if the beneficiary is a minor or if the donor wants flexibility to provide for beneficiaries who might not even be born at the time that the trust is created (e.g. grandchildren).

They can also be used to mitigate inheritance tax by placing property from the donor's estate on death into a discretionary trust. Generally, a trust is set up to protect the property should the beneficiary be mentally incapable, should the property needs to be sold to pay for long term care, or should there be a bankruptcy or divorce.

### What is a trust?

A trust is set up by a "settlor" who instructs that particular assets are removed from his/her ownership and put aside for use by a "beneficiary" in the trust; the "trustees" have control of the assets. Trust assets can be in any form: real or personal, tangible or intangible. Often they are shares, cash or property.

Legally no formalities are required in order to create a Trust. It can be oral, although the trust must be written when land is involved. In any event, a formal written trust deed helps to avoid any future misunderstandings.

The role of the trustee is very important. The trustees are the *legal* owners of the property but they cannot use the property as if it were their own personal property. They use and keep the property secure only for the benefit of the beneficiaries.

The beneficiaries are the *beneficial* owners of the trust property who either immediately or eventually, will receive the income from the trust property, if any, or the property itself.

The extent of an individual beneficiary's interest depends upon the wording of the trust deed. For example, of two beneficiaries one might be entitled to the bank account interest income only but the other might be allowed the entire capital on his 25th birthday.

In the U.K. a distinction is currently made between two main types of Trust. Under a Qualifying Interest in Possession (QIIP) trust, a beneficiary is entitled to the income as well as the underlying asset (property) on death. Under a "Discretionary" or, since Finance Act 2006, "Mainstream" Trust, no one is entitled to the income or assets. Rather it is at the discretion of the trustees as to how both are distributed dependent upon the terms of the trust Deed.

## Trusts in Belgium

Belgium is a civil law country and it does not have the concept of trust. However, in the Private International Law Code, the trust is recognised as being a legal concept in common law countries. The Code defines trusts in similar terms as the Hague Convention on Trusts; "a trust is a legal relationship created by an act of the founder (settlor) or by a judicial decision, whereby assets have been placed under the control of a trustee for the benefit of a beneficiary or for a specified purpose".

What is important is that the law recognises that trust assets constitute a separate fund, distinct from the settlor's and the trustee's own estates. Title to the trust assets stands in the name of the trustee with the power and the duty to manage, employ or dispose of these assets in accordance with the terms of the trust and the special duties imposed upon him by law; he is accountable in respect of this duty.

The Code confirms the freedom of the settlor to choose the law of a jurisdiction that has a trust concept. A trust can still not be set up under Belgian law as there is no possibility to split legal and beneficial ownership. At the same time, the Code sets limits to the settlor's freedom: Belgian public order, the forced heirship rules and *fraus legis*.

## Trusts in Belgian tax law

Belgium may acknowledge the existence of the trust, but that does not mean that there are any rules in the tax law governing trusts. To determine the tax regime governing a trust in Belgium, one has to analyse the various components of the trust arrangement in terms of Belgian civil law. Belgian tax law does, indeed, follow civil law. The different transactions and legal relationships as well as the respective rights and obligations of settlor, trustee and beneficiary must be translated into terms of Belgian civil law before the Belgian tax rules can be applied.

In general, commentators analyse the trust in the light of two extreme versions of the trust: the irrevocable and discretionary trust or the fixed interest trust. Their conclusion generally is that an irrevocable and discretionary trust is not transparent, while a fixed interest trust is transparent.

### An irrevocable and discretionary trust

If he sets up an irrevocable and discretionary trust, the settlor transfers the trust assets to the trustee who has full discretionary powers to decide if he gives any trust assets or income from the trust assets, and to whom and when he gives it to them. The trustee is the legal owner of the assets, with a duty to use them on behalf of the beneficiaries, but the beneficiaries have no right or no control over the trust assets or the income from the trust assets. When they receive anything from the trustee this would be a gratuity.

The **settlor** waives all rights to the trust assets or the income from these assets. He is not entitled to any income or any control over the assets, and he abandons these assets, the income or the control with no hope of recovering them. In general, there can be no gift tax when he transfers the assets to the trustee, and since the assets are not in his estate anymore, inheritance tax will not be due. Since he does not have any right to the income, he cannot be liable to income tax, subject to some anti-avoidance rules (see below).

The **trustee** holds title to the trust assets and collects the income from those assets, he is the one who may be liable to income tax in his country of residence.

The **beneficiaries** have no rights at all vis-à-vis the trustee. If they receive anything at all, that is a gratuity given by the trustee, on which no gift tax or income tax is due.

This analysis was confirmed by the tax authorities in a decision in 2004. However, they added the proviso that when the beneficiary received anything at all from the trust, that would be liable to inheritance tax. They refer to the provision for a third party rule in the inheritance tax code (see p. 77). That rule states that when someone receives a benefit from a contract between the deceased and a third party (think of an insurance policy), that benefit is liable to inheritance tax.

Their conclusion is that inheritance would be due anytime the trustee pays a benefit, even years after the settlor's death and an inheritance tax return would need to be filed every time. This is contested since the trust deed is, typically, not a contract.

### A fixed interest trust

If the trust is fixed, some or all transactions or relationships will be treated as transparent for tax purposes. There are many variations of this type of trust, but in its most basic form, the settlor appoints a bank as a trustee to hold money to the benefit of himself and his family.

In an accumulation trust, the trustee accumulates the income to pay it out to beneficiaries at some time in the future.

The *settlor* may still have a right to the income, and continue to be liable to income tax. There would be no gift tax, since the settlor has not given away his assets, the trustee holds them in accordance with his instructions to pass them on at some time in the future. Moreover, inheritance tax may be due when the settlor dies, but that depends on the situation.

The *trustee* must manage the trust assets and distribute the income, and the trust assets, in accordance with the settlor's instructions. He holds the assets as a nominee for the settlor or in his own name with a personal duty to make payments to the beneficiaries.

The *beneficiaries* are clearly given the right to receive a specific fixed interest in the trust. Whether and when they are liable to inheritance tax depends on the situation. In an accumulation trust they might not receive any entitlement until years after the settlor's death. However, if they receive an entitlement more than three years before his death, inheritance tax may not be due.

## Estate planning with trusts

The trust is the most flexible way of planning the management and transfer of an estate.

### Practical limitations

The most important limitation are the forced heirship rules, which protect the settlor's heirs by reserving a part of his estate to certain protected heirs. These protected heirs are the children and grandchildren, the surviving spouse, and the parents and grandparents of the settlor. However, only the forced heirs can exercise their rights to recover the trust assets. Nobody else can exercise these rights and if they do nothing, and respect the settlor's instructions, nobody else can do anything about it, not even the tax authorities.

In any event, a trust should not be used to hold Belgian real property, since the transfer of ownership and rights in rem on real estate requires the registration of the transfer deed in the mortgage registry, and the transfer of property to the trust estate would create a problem. This problem could be circumvented by holding Belgian real property via a special purpose company.

Given the analysis of the discretionary trust, this seems to be the most obvious vehicle for tax efficient estate planning.

### Planning an estate through a fixed interest trust

A fixed interest trust can also be used for estate planning. However, since the tax authorities can simply see through the setup, this requires more caution on the part of the settlor. The problem is that there are many forms of fixed interest trusts.

In its most basic form, the trust is simply transparent and the settlor appoints a trustee to hold money for himself, and upon his death for the benefit of his family. During his lifetime, he will continue to be liable to income tax, and when he dies, the beneficiaries will be liable to inheritance tax. The value on which the inheritance tax will be due is either the capital paid out by the trustee or the net present value of the future payments.

In an accumulation trust, the trustee accumulates the income to pay it out to beneficiaries at some time in the future. This can create problems to determine who will pay inheritance tax. The settlor may not have any entitlement to income, and the beneficiaries may not even know that income is being accumulated for their benefit.

When the beneficiaries receive a payment from the trust, they would need to file a new inheritance tax return completing the earlier one to declare the benefit under the provision for a third party rule in the inheritance tax code. The inheritance tax will be calculated at the rate for everything they received.

Tax planning may be possible by making sure that the transfer from the settlor to the beneficiary via the trustee qualifies as a donation between the settlor to the beneficiary. If this is done before a notary gift tax will be due at the lower rates on movables. If the donation is formalised before a Dutch or Swiss notary, inheritance tax will be due unless the settlor lives for another three years.

### An irrevocable and discretionary trust to plan your estate

Based on the 2004 decision of the tax authorities, an irrevocable and discretionary trust appears to be the perfect solution for inheritance tax planning. There is no gift tax on the transfer to the trustee, there is no income tax on the income from the trust assets and because the payments to the beneficiaries are gratuities, no inheritance tax is due.

There is, however, the position of the tax administration (in 2004) that any distributions from a discretionary trust would be liable to inheritance tax based on the contract for a third party rule. That position is contested as the trust deed is not an agreement. However, this decision is the starting point for the Ruling Committee.

There are a few considerations, though, to be kept in mind.

First, if the trustee is based in a tax haven, the settlor may have to continue to pay income tax on the income from the trust assets.

The tax authorities can, indeed, disregard a transfer of certain income-producing assets or cash to a non-resident taxpayer in a tax haven.

Such transfer cannot be opposed by the tax authorities (for income tax purposes only), unless the taxpayer proves that the transaction meets legitimate financial or economic needs, or that he has received valuable consideration that generates income that is subject to a tax substantially equivalent to the tax which would have been due in the absence of a transfer. This anti-avoidance rule only works for income tax purposes and only against the taxpayer who has transferred the assets.

Furthermore, for a trust to be truly irrevocable and discretionary, the settlor must abandon any entitlement to the trust property and to the income of the trust assets, as well as control over the trust property, without any hope of recovering the trust assets, the income they generate or the control over the way they are used.

As for the beneficiary, he does not pay income tax if the payments from the trustee are effectively gratuities. That means that he must not have any right to the trust assets or to the income of the trust assets received by the trustee. If the beneficiary receives an annuity from a corporate trustee, the interest component in that annuity is taxable at a flat rate of 25%, to be increased with the municipal surcharge (usually between 6 and 9%, a 6% municipal surcharge means 26.5% tax). The interest component is determined by the income tax code as 3% of the initial capital; the initial capital must be determined by an actuarial calculation.

There are only a few advance rulings given by the Ruling Committee on trusts. These show that its members are making a serious effort to understand the concept of the trust, but that they are making sure they do not get it wrong. They will look at any indications that the trust might be "partially influenceable" and, therefore, "not entirely discretionary".

# Foundations

The private foundation is the form of special purpose fund that is closest to a trust. It was originally set up to allow Belgian entrepreneurs to create "certificates" of the shares of their company. This allowed them to split legal and the economic ownership of the shares which enables them to transmit their business.

By incorporating a foundation, one can split off an estate for a (disinterested) purpose that continues after his death. This can be done to maintain an art collection, to support the development of a region, to create a scientific or cultural prize, to preserve an estate of a historic building. The private foundation can be an appropriate structure to provide care for a disabled child after the parents' death.

Following the commotion about the foundation set up by Queen Fabiola, the government announced that the law would be adapted so that the private foundation could no longer have potential for tax evasion. Private foundations should only be used for charitable purposes..

## The legal framework

The private foundation can be incorporated during the founder's lifetime in a notarised deed. It can also be set up upon death, in accordance with a will drafted by a notary.

A private foundation has no members or shareholders and no general meeting of members or shareholders. There is only a board of directors consisting of at least three directors.

It is essential that the foundation does not give any direct financial benefit to its founders, directors or to any other person. It may distribute funds to the designated beneficiaries if that is its purpose, e.g. a private foundation set up to provide for the maintenance of a (disabled) child or for the welfare and education of certain relatives.

It is only when the founder has no protected heirs that he can leave his entire estate to his foundation. If he has any children, a spouse or parents, he can only use the disposable part of his estate.

The founder must remember that he is definitively relinquishing the assets he earmarks for the foundation. He cannot get them back.

Moreover, winding up a private foundation can only be decided by a court to ensure that the assets are given for a disinterested purpose as indicated in the incorporation deed.

There is one situation where the founder (or after his death, his successors) can recover assets which the founder had provided to achieve the goal of the foundation. The articles of incorporation must expressly provide for the possibility of the assets reverting to the founder or his successors and the purpose of the foundation must have been achieved.

## Advantages for tax savings

The tax regime of a private foundation makes it interesting for estate planning.

### A donation to the foundation

Any donation to a foundation for a value in excess of €100,000 (of movable and of real property), and both inter vivos or by will requires the prior authorization of the Minister of Justice. If the Minister does not respond within three months, the donation is deemed authorized. This authorization is not required for hand to hand donations or bank donations.

When a person (an individual or a body corporate) makes a contribution (at the time of the incorporation or afterwards) or a donation to a private foundation, gift tax is due at 7% (in the whole country) for both movable and real property. If gift tax is paid, no inheritance tax will be due anymore.

If the founder finds 7% gift tax too much, he can opt for a hand to hand donation, a bank gift or a donation before a Dutch or Swiss notary. These are valid alternatives that do not trigger gift tax. However, if the donor dies within three years, inheritance tax will still be due under the three year rule, but the inheritance tax rate is very low as well (see below).

### The foundation inherits

A foundation can receive bequests. Bequests over €100,000 require a prior ministerial authorization.

In Flanders, the inheritance tax rate is 8.8%, and in Wallonia 7%. In Brussels, the basic rate is 25% but if the private foundation has obtained federal approval to issue tax certificates for donations, the rate in Brussels is 12.5%.

These low inheritance tax rates create interesting estate planning options. A childless uncle can set up a private foundation with a few assets and some cash. During his lifetime, he can keep the estate for his own needs. He can bequeath the rest of his estate to the foundation, and the foundation will inherit the entire estate and pay the low inheritance tax rates. The foundation can then use his estate for the intended purpose, e.g. give to nieces and nephews, keep or maintain a family property, donate to charities, etc...

### Distributions to the beneficiaries

During the lifetime of the founder, benefits granted by the foundation to the beneficiaries designated in the articles of incorporation do not attract gift tax.

Moreover, benefits granted to the designated beneficiaries after the death of the founder are not liable to inheritance tax either. The Ruling Committee has decided that the contracts in favour of a third party rule does not apply; the incorporation deed is a unilateral act and not a contract. Inheritance tax will only be due if no gift tax had been paid at the time of the contribution or donation to the foundation and the founder dies within three years.

### Winding up the foundation to recover assets

As mentioned above, the articles may allow the founder or his successors to recover the assets when the private foundation has achieved its purpose. The Ruling Committee has taken the position that if the assets revert to the founder himself, no tax is due. The assets will fall into his estate and be liable to inheritance tax when he dies.

However, if the assets revert to his heirs, they will have to file a new inheritance tax return and pay additional inheritance tax.

## Foreign foundations

Even if the Belgian government decides to change the law, the rules set out above would still apply if a founder were to use a foreign foundation. In that respect, it is interesting to note that Liechtenstein is part of the European Economic Area and that an *Anstalt,* the

Liechtenstein foundation, could receive gifts that are subject to gift tax at 7%.

Not many countries have foundations; that is why Frenchmen Bernard Arnault, the CEO of LVMH chose to set up a Belgian foundation to keep his shareholding together until 2023 when all his children will be 25 and able to fend for themselves.

# PLAN FOR YOURSELF

When we all get older, there is a risk that we may not have the good health to manage our affairs or to express our wishes about health care and discontinuing medical care.

## A LEGAL GUARDIAN

When you are no longer able to manage our estate, the justice of the peace can appoint a legal guardian who will do this in your place. He will decide who will have power of attorney for your finances, and you may want to have a say in the matter, in advance.

A legal guardian (*voorlopig bewindvoerder / administrateur provisoire*) can be appointed to protect the estate of someone who is not capable of looking after his affairs due to his medical condition. Dementia is not necessary; memory lapses or a continual lack of interest for financial and money matters can justify the appointment, even a drop in the attention required to manage a large fortune.

The justice of the peace can take that decision at his own initiative, e.g. when a physician draws his attention to the situation of their patient. It is more common for a relative (a spouse, child, ...) to request the appointment with a doctor's certificate.

If you want to have a say in the appointment of a legal guardian while you are still in good health, you can make a statement before the justice of the peace or a notary. This statement is recorded in a central register where the justice of the peace can see that you have made such statement. He will have to take account of your wishes, unless there are good reasons not to do so, *e.g.* when the person you appoint is not capable of looking after your affairs.

If you do not appoint a legal guardian, the justice of the peace appoints a close relative: a parent, the spouse, the registered partner or even the live-in partner. The relatives can make suggestions, but the justice of the peace is not obliged to follow these. He will talk with the person in question as well as with the people with whom he lives.

The staff of the institution where the protected person lives cannot be appointed.

The justice of the peace decides what powers the legal guardian will have, and that is not something you can decide in your statement. Even if the justice of the peace gives him full powers, the guardian cannot purchase property, take out loans, give a mortgage, or accept donations or bequests, sell belongings or properties without the authorisation of the justice of the peace.

The protected person himself cannot make any donations anymore without the approval of the justice of the peace; he will refuse that if the donation would impoverish him. The justice of the peace will not, however, forbid him to make a will, as long as he is sound of mind.

The justice of the peace can also appoint a supervisor, and in your statement you can designate the supervisor. His main task is to express the wishes of the protected person and to supervise the guardian. The guardian will have to report regularly to the supervisor.

# A LIVING WILL

If you do not have a living will, your loved ones will be left with the difficult decision whether to continue or discontinue medical treatment. Continue medical treatment may require artificial feeding and respiration, and medical interventions, at great cost to your estate. When there is no living will, such life-and-death decisions can rip a family apart.

Since Belgium authorised euthanasia, you can draw up a living will that is limited to request euthanasia and to express your wishes as to the final stages of treatment.

Any adult can draw up a living will (called "advance directives") instructing a physician to perform euthanasia if he ensures that the patient suffers from a serious and incurable disorder caused by illness or accident, that he is no longer conscious and that this condition is irreversible given the current state of medical science.

There is an official model of a living will (a translation in English can be found on p. 222).

In your living will you can designate one or more persons. Their role is not to take decisions on behalf of the patient but to inform the physician of his instructions. The living will is dated and signed with two witnesses (one of them must not have any financial interest) and two appointees. There is also a procedure for drafting a living will for someone who is not capable to draft it but who can still designate someone to do so for him.

We would recommend drafting a living will in French or Dutch in accordance with this model, in particular if you want to register it with the commune. The living will is then lodged with the Ministry of Public Health and the basic information is recorded in a database. The physician who has a patient who cannot express his will must access the database to find his living will. The information to which he has access includes: the name, sex and main residence of the patient, the date and object of the advance directives and the contact details of the appointees.

A physician may refuse to perform euthanasia, but he must inform the patient or his appointee so that they can look for another physician. The physician who performs euthanasia in accordance with a living will does not commit a criminal offence if he ensures that the patient has a serious and incurable disorder, that he has lost consciousness and that the condition is irreversible. The physician cannot take his decision on his own; he must consult with another physician. Physicians may impose additional conditions before performing euthanasia.

More information can be obtained from Association pour le Droit de Mourir dans la Dignité, rue du Président 55, 1050 Brussels (info@admd.be, phone: 02 502 04 85,), or Recht op Waardig Sterven, Lange Gasthuisstraat 35-37, 2000 Antwerpen (info@rws.be, phone: 03 272 51 63).

# PRACTICAL PLANNING

We would advise you to set up a Personal Affairs Checklist to keep track of your personal affairs and documents. Investing a little time now to complete the checklist could save your spouse, partner, children, relatives or friends a great deal of time and expense in the future.

A Personal Affairs Checklist is not a will and should not contain instructions about what should be done with your money or possessions. It is a record of where your key personal records, assets and papers can be located. On p. 207, we give a model of such a checklist.

When completed, the checklist will contain confidential information. We recommend that you keep the form somewhere safe, maybe in your bank or with your accountant or solicitor; or you give the form to someone you trust to hold for you in a safe place.

We would suggest that you combine this with your own Personal Affairs Box or Personal Affairs Binder (PAB).

While you are completing your Personal Affairs Checklist, just put all important documents and records in a file or binder: your marriage book (*trouwboekje / livret de mariage*) ; a copy of your marriage contract (the original stays with the notary) ; property deeds for property outside Belgium ; a copy of purchase deeds for property in Belgium, France, … ; other notarised deeds (e.g. donations) ; insurance policies, etc …

# ANNEXES

The following models can be downloaded on www.taxation.be under the heading Estate Planning

        Brussels Capital Region: Gift Tax
        Brussels Capital Region: Inheritance Tax
        Flanders: Gift Tax
        Flanders: Inheritance Tax
        Wallonia: Gift Tax
        Wallonia: Inheritance Tax

# PERSONAL AFFAIRS CHECKLIST

For **Name**
   Address

In the event of my death or incapacity due to sudden illness,

## please contact:

| | | |
|---|---|---|
| Name<br>Address<br><br>Phone:<br>E-mail | | |

**Family / relatives**
**Spouse / Civil partner / partner**

| | |
|---|---|
| Name<br>Date of birth<br>Address | |

Children

| | |
|---|---|
| Name<br>Date of birth<br>Address | |

| | |
|---|---|
| Name<br>Date of birth<br>Address | |

| | |
|---|---|
| Name<br>Date of birth<br>Address | |

   If you have no children: list your living parents or other living relatives

| Name<br>Date of birth<br>Address<br><br>Relationship | |
| --- | --- |

| Name<br>Date of birth<br>Address<br><br>Relationship | |
| --- | --- |

| Name<br>Date of birth<br>Address<br><br>Relationship | |
| --- | --- |

| Name<br>Date of birth<br>Address<br><br>Relationship | |
| --- | --- |

| Name<br>Date of birth<br>Address<br><br>Relationship | |
| --- | --- |

| Name<br>Date of birth<br>Address<br><br>Relationship | |
| --- | --- |

# My advisers:

|  | Doctor | Priest/Clergyman |
|---|---|---|
| Name<br>Address<br><br>Phone:<br>E-mail | | |

|  | Undertaker | Lawyer |
|---|---|---|
| Name<br>Address<br><br>Phone:<br>E-mail | | |

|  | Notary | Accountant |
|---|---|---|
| Name<br>Address<br><br>Phone:<br>E-mail | | |

Other Advisers

| Name<br>Address<br><br>Phone:<br>E-mail | | |
|---|---|---|

# Important contacts

**Employer**
Details of employment
Company Name
Address
Employment Reference Phone
Please contact

**Pension**
Social security / National Insurance or PPS number
Address

Please contact

**Pension schemes**
Name
Please contact
My reference number
PAB

Name
Please contact
My reference number
PAB

**Directorships**
Company Name
Address

Company Name
Address

**Associations, Clubs and Societies**
Association
Address
Contact

Association
Address
Contact

# My Will(s)

**1. in** ..................................................................................(country)

| | |
|---|---|
| The original of my Will is with | |
| Date | |
| is drawn up by | |
| copy in PAB | # |
| Address | |
| | |
| Phone: | |
| E-mail | |
| the executors are | |

**2. in** ..................................................................................(country)

| | |
|---|---|
| The original of my Will is with | |
| Date | |
| is drawn up by | |
| copy in PAB | # |
| Address | |
| | |
| Phone: | |
| E-mail | |
| the executors are | |

**3. in** ..................................................................................(country)

| | |
|---|---|
| The original of my Will is with | |
| Date | |
| is drawn up by | |
| copy in PAB | # |
| Address | |
| | |
| Phone: | |
| E-mail | |
| the executors are | |

My wishes regarding care of **pets** may be found: PAB #

My **Birth** certificate may be found
PAB #

My Marriage Certificate may be found
PAB #

Other documents relating to marriage may be found
PAB #

**Power of Attorney for me is held by**

A "Living Will" declaration to family and doctors may be found in my
PAB #

Medical Research Bequests/Donor Card may be found (eyes, kidneys, etc.) PAB #

**Funeral Arrangements**

A note outlining my preferences may be found: PAB #

Tomb Plot
    plot reference number

Title Deeds may be found

# Properties

**Main Residence**

| | |
|---|---|
| Address | |
| | |
| Phone | |
| Location of Deeds* | |
| PAB | # |
| Co-owner / Joint owner | |
| Mortgage Lender (Name & Address) | |
| Account Number | |

Other properties

| | |
|---|---|
| Address | |
| | |
| Phone | |
| Location of Deeds* | |
| PAB | # |
| Co-owner / Joint owner | |
| Mortgage Lender (Name & Address) | |
| Account Number | |

| | |
|---|---|
| Address | |
| | |
| Phone | |
| Location of Deeds* | |
| PAB | # |
| Co-owner / Joint owner | |
| Mortgage Lender (Name & Address) | |
| Account Number | |

* for Belgian properties, the deeds are always kept by the notary; keep a copy of the purchase deed and mortgage deed in the PAB

**Rented properties**

| | |
|---|---|
| Address<br><br>Phone<br>Rental agreement: PAB<br>Contact owner at<br>Name & Address<br>Phone:<br>Contact manager<br>Name & Address<br>Phone: | # |

| | |
|---|---|
| Address<br><br>Phone<br>Rental agreement: PAB<br>Contact owner at<br>Name & Address<br>Phone:<br>Contact manager<br>Name & Address<br>Phone: | # |

**Time share**

| | |
|---|---|
| Address<br><br>Property deeds: PAB<br>Contact manager<br>Name & Address<br>Phone: | # |

| | |
|---|---|
| Address<br><br>Property deeds: PAB<br>Contact manager<br>Name & Address<br>Phone: | # |

# Account(s)

with Banks, Building Society, Post Office, Credit Union, etc.

I have  (number) accounts
These accounts are held at the institution(s) indicated below

**1. in** ....................................................................................(country)

| | |
|---|---|
| Institution<br>Address<br><br>Contact:<br>Phone:<br>Account No.<br>Type of account * | |

| | |
|---|---|
| Account No.<br>Type of account * | |

| | |
|---|---|
| Account No.<br>Type of account * | |

| | |
|---|---|
| Account No.<br>Type of account * | |

| | |
|---|---|
| Account No.<br>Type of account * | |

* Type of account: current account, savings account, investment
account

| Institution<br>Address<br><br>Contact:<br>Phone:<br>Account No.<br>Type of account * | |
| --- | --- |

| Account No.<br>Type of account * | |
| --- | --- |

| Account No.<br>Type of account * | |
| --- | --- |

**2. in** .....................................................................(country)

| Institution<br>Address<br><br>Contact:<br>Phone:<br>Account No.<br>Type of account * | |
| --- | --- |

| Account No.<br>Type of account * | |
| --- | --- |

| Account No.<br>Type of account * | |
| --- | --- |

**3. in** ....................................................................(country)

| Institution<br>Address<br><br>Contact:<br>Phone:<br>Account No.<br>Type of account * | |

| Account No.<br>Type of account * | |

**4. in** ....................................................................(country)

| Institution<br>Address<br><br>Contact:<br>Phone:<br>Account No.<br>Type of account * | |

| Account No.<br>Type of account * | |

**Credit Cards**

| Type of Card | Credit Card No | Via bank |
| --- | --- | --- |
|  |  |  |
|  |  |  |
|  |  |  |
|  |  |  |

# Investments

(shares, unit-trusts, premium bonds, national savings certificates, etc.)

| Type | May be found or held on investment account |
|------|--------------------------------------------|
|      |                                            |
|      |                                            |
|      |                                            |
|      |                                            |
|      |                                            |

# Insurance policies

e.g. Life, Car, Home, Health

| Insurance Broker Address<br><br>Contact<br>Phone<br>Email | |
|------------------------------------------------------------|--|

| Insurance Broker Address<br><br>Contact<br>Phone<br>Email | |
|------------------------------------------------------------|--|

Insurance company

| Insurance Company<br>Address<br><br>Phone | |
|---|---|

| Policy Type<br>Policy Number<br>PAB | |
| # | |

| Policy Type<br>Policy Number<br>PAB | |
| # | |

| Policy Type<br>Policy Number<br>PAB | |
| # | |

| Insurance Company<br>Address<br><br>Phone | |
|---|---|

| Policy Type<br>Policy Number<br>PAB | |
| # | |

| Policy Type<br>Policy Number<br>PAB | |
| # | |

| Policy Type<br>Policy Number<br>PAB | |
| # | |

# Other assets

My **deed/safe box** may be found

The key may be found
Key Number

The access codes to my **computer** are to be found in an envelope,
cross-signed by me,
which is held at

Jewellery

Other assets

Details may be found

# Major Debts

## Creditor

| | |
|---|---|
| Name<br>Address<br><br>Phone<br>Location of contract<br>PAB | <br><br><br><br><br>#  |

| | |
|---|---|
| Name<br>Address<br><br>Phone<br>Location of contract<br>PAB | <br><br><br><br><br>#  |

| | |
|---|---|
| Name<br>Address<br><br>Phone<br>Location of contract<br>PAB | <br><br><br><br><br>#  |

# Other Information

(Not covered by any section above)

Date completed
PAC to be held at

# A LIVING WILL

This model is a translation of the form that can be found on www.taxation.be under Estate Planning.

**MANDATARY INFORMATION**

### Object of the advance directives

[ Mr / Mrs ] [ your full name ]

(*)     request that, in case [ he/she ] is not capable to express [ his/her ] will, a doctor performs euthanasia if all conditions of the law of 28 May 2002 on euthanasia are met

(*)     reconfirms the advance directives re euthanasia that have been drafted on [ date ] [1]

(*)     revises the advance directives re euthanasia that have been drafted on [ date ] [1]

(*)     withdraws the advance directives re euthanasia that have been drafted on [ date ] [1]

### Personal data of the applicant.

My personal data are:
- main residence
- full address
- identification number in the national register
- date and place of birth

### Characteristics of the advance directives

This declaration has been made freely and consciously. It has been approved by the signature of two witnesses and where appropriate, (a) person(s) of confidence
I wish that these advance directives be respected.

**The witnesses**
The witnesses in the presence of whom I wrote these advance directives are:

1)      name and first name
        main residence
        full address
        identification number in the national register
        phone number
        date and place of birth
        possible family ties

2)      name and first name
        main residence
        full address
        identification number in the national register
        phone number
        date and place of birth
        possible family ties

## OPTIONAL INFORMATION

**Designation of trusted person(s) ("appointees')**
As trusted person(s), whom I wish be immediately informed if I find myself in a situation in which the advance directives might need to be applied and whom I want to see involved during the process I designate in order of preference:

1)      name and first name
        main residence
        full address
identification number in the national register

        phone number
        date and place of birth
        possible family ties

2)      name and first name
        main residence
        full address
        identification number in the national register
        phone number
        date and place of birth

possible family ties
**Information to be mentioned by the person who is physically incapable of drafting and signing advance directives.**

The reason why I am unable to physically write and sign these advance directives is as follows: [      ].
By way of evidence, I attach a medical certificate.

I have appointed [ *name and first name* ] to record these advance directives in writing.

The personal data of the above-mentioned persons are:
      main residence
      full address
      identification number in the national register
      phone number
      date and place of birth
      possible family ties

These advance directives have been written in [ *number* ] signed copies which are held [ *either at a place or with a person* ].

Done at [ *place* ], this [ *date* ] [*signature and stamp of the commune* ]

Done at [ *place* ], this [ *date* ] [ *your signature* ]

Date and signature of the person designated in case of a permanent physical disability of the applicant [1]

Date and signature of the two witnesses

Date and signature of the person(s) designated [1]

[ *for each date and signature mention*) (quality and name)


[*] delete as appropriate
[1] if applicable
[2] the data under 1) are indicated for each designated appointee.

# A HANDWRITTEN WILL

This is my last will and testament

The undersigned [ *your name* ] born in [ *your place of birth* ] on [ *your date of birth* ]

(optional) and married to [ *name of spouse* ] born in [ *place of birth* ] on [ *date of birth* ] with whom I was married at [ *place* ], on [ *date* ], without having signed a marriage contract, and with whom I established my first habitual residence after our marriage at [ *place* ]

and currently residing at [ *your residence* ]

declare to make my last will and testament as follows.

I revoke any other last wills and testaments which I may have made in the past.

(optional) I appoint [ *my spouse / x* ] as my general legatee, and I bequeath [ *to him / her* ] the highest disposable portion of my estate, in full ownership and in usufruct of all my real and personal property at the time of my death, as such percentage shall be determined by the law at that time, without prejudice to [ *his/her* ] hereditary rights to the usufruct,

(in Flanders) and in particular, I wish that my [ *spouse* ] receives my share in the family home in [ *place* ].

I release my [ *spouse* ] from giving a security for the usufruct. To the extent that the law will permit me, I deny my children and descendants the right to request conversion of usufruct.

If my [ *spouse* ] predeceases me, or dies at the same time as me, I appoint my child(ren) [ *Name(s)* ] as my general legatees.

I leave my [*house/apartment/...*] at [ *address* ] to [ *name of beneficiary* ] born on [ *date of birth* ].

I leave [ *other assets* ] to [ *name of beneficiary* ] born on [ *date of birth* ].

In case my spouse and I were to die before our children reach majority, I wish to appoint as their guardian [ *Name* ] residing at [ *place* ], and in case he is not able to accept this appointment, I wish to appoint as their guardian [ *Name* ] residing at [ *place* ].

I wish that my remains be cremated and I leave the decision about the scattering of my ashes to my heirs

Handwritten in full, dated and signed by me,

Done in [ *place* ] on [ *date* ].

*Signature*

# DOCUMENTS FOR A HAND-TO-HAND DONATION

Nancy Sinatra
Rue Middelbourg 312
1160 Brussels


                              Miss Francine Sinatra
                              De Coninckplein 10 b 13
                              2000 Antwerpen

REGISTERED MAIL WITH
RETURN RECEIPT MESSAGE

                              Brussels, [_date_]


Dear Nancy,

Can you meet me on [_date_] at the Brussels branch of [_bank_] Bank at [_address_], I would like to make a donation to you.


Yours sincerely,


(signature)

Nancy Sinatra

Francine Sinatra
De Coninckplein 10 b 13
2000 Antwerpen


Mrs Nancy Sinatra
Rue Middelbourg 312
1160 Brussels

REGISTERED MAIL WITH
RETURN RECEIPT MESSAGE

Brussels, [_date_]


Dear Mom,

Thank you for your donation on [_date_] at the Brussels branch of
[_bank_] Bank at [_address_].

I accept this donation with gratitude.


Yours sincerely,



(signature)
Francine Sinatra

# A DONATION BY BANK TRANSFER

Tom Jones
Rue Général Jacques 12/34
1000 Brussels

> Mr Sonny Jones
> Rue Hergé 123
> 1348 Louvain-la-Neuve

REGISTERED MAIL WITH
RETURN RECEIPT MESSAGE

> Brussels, [_date_]

Dear Sonny,

On [_date_], I will transfer €10,000 to your account nr ___-_____-__by way of donation.

I wish to transfer the full ownership of these funds under the following conditions ...

Please confirm that you can accept these conditions.

Yours sincerely,


 (signature)

Tom Jones

Sonny Jones
Rue Hergé 123
1348 Louvain-la-Neuve

Mr Tom Jones
Rue Général Jacques 12/34
1000 Brussels

REGISTERED MAIL WITH
RETURN RECEIPT MESSAGE

Brussels, [_date_]

Dear Dad,

On [_date_], I received your donation of €10,000 on my bank account
___-_____-__ as announced in your letter of [_date_], also on my
bank account.

I accept these donations with gratitude.

Moreover, I undertake to comply with the conditions you put in your
letter, that is:

Yours sincerely,


(signature)

Sonny Jones

# A PRIVATE DONATION AGREEMENT
DONATION MADE ON [_date_] AND [_date_]

Between      Tom Jones, residing at Rue Général Jacques 12/34, 1000 Brussels, the donor

And      Sonny Jones, residing at rue Hergé 123, 1348 Louvain-la-Neuve, the beneficiary

Tom Jones, donor, hereby declares having made a donation by transfer from his bank account in the amount of €10,000 to the account nr ___-_____-__ of Sonny Jones. The donor declares having transferred the full ownership of these amounts to be used by the beneficiary to purchase the property at [_address_].

The beneficiary confirms having received this amount on bank account ___-_____-__ on [_date_] and confirms accepting this donation.

The beneficiary declares having used or undertakes to use these amounts for the purchase of said property. Moreover, he undertakes that if these funds are not used for the purchase of said property, they will be returned to the donor at first demand.

Optional: The beneficiary agrees that in case he dies before the donor, the funds, or the real property rights purchased with the funds, will be returned in full ownership to the donor, in accordance with articles 951 and 952 of the Civil code.

Optional: The beneficiary undertakes that in case he contracts marriage, he will sign a marriage contract so that the funds donated or the real property purchased with the funds will not become community property.

Done in Brussels, on [__date__], in two copies, and each party acknowledges having received a copy.

_____          _____

Tom Jones                    Sonny Jones

# Brussels Capital Region: Gift Tax

Gift tax on **movables** is calculated at the flat rate of 3% between (grand)parents and (grand)children, spouses and registered partners, and 7% for donations to anyone else.

Gift tax on **real property** is calculated on the value of the donation

| On the band between | | | Rate | Tax on previous bands |
|---|---|---|---|---|
| **1 Direct line, spouses, registered partners** | | | | |
| €0 | - | €50 000 | 3% | |
| €50 000 | - | €100 000 | 8% | + €1 500 |
| €100 000 | - | €175 000 | 9% | + €5 500 |
| €175 0000 | - | €250 000 | 18% | + €12 250 |
| €250 000 | - | €500 000 | 24% | + €25 750 |
| over €500 000 | | | 30% | + €85 750 |
| **2 Between brothers and sisters** | | | | |
| €0 | - | €12 500 | 20% | |
| €12 500 | - | €25 000 | 25% | + €2 500 |
| €25 000 | - | €50 000 | 30% | + €5 625 |
| €50 000 | - | €100 000 | 40% | + €13 125 |
| €100 000 | - | €175 000 | 55% | + €33 125 |
| €175 000 | - | €250 000 | 60% | + €74 375 |
| Over €250 000 | | | 65% | + €119 375 |
| **3. Between uncles/aunts and nephews/nieces** | | | | |
| €0 | - | €50 000 | 35% | |
| €50 000 | - | €100 000 | 50% | + €17 500 |
| €100 000 | - | €175 000 | 65% | + €42 500 |
| over €175 000 | | | 70% | + €87 500 |
| **4 Between other persons** | | | | |
| €0 | - | €50 000 | 40% | |
| €50 000 | - | €75 000 | 55% | + €20 000 |
| €75 000 | - | €175 000 | 60% | + €33 750 |
| over €175 000 | | | 80% | + €98 750 |

Donations to non-profit associations and foundations (in Belgium or in the European Economic Area): 7%.

# Brussels Capital Region: Inheritance Tax

Inheritance tax is calculated, for each heir separately, on his share

| On the band between | | | Rate | Tax on previous bands |
|---|---|---|---|---|
| **1 Direct line, spouses, registered partners** | | | | |
| €0 | - | €50 000 | 3% | |
| €50 000 | - | €100 000 | 8% | + €1 500 |
| €100 000 | - | €175 000 | 9% | + €5 500 |
| €175 0000 | - | €250 000 | 18% | + €12 250 |
| €250 000 | - | €500 000 | 24% | + €25 750 |
| over €500 000 | | | 30% | + €85 750 |
| **2 Between brothers and sisters** | | | | |
| €0 | - | €12 500 | 20% | |
| €12 500 | - | €25 000 | 25% | + €2 500 |
| €25 000 | - | €50 000 | 30% | + €5 625 |
| €50 000 | - | €100 000 | 40% | + €13 125 |
| €100 000 | - | €175 000 | 55% | + €33 125 |
| €175 000 | - | €250 000 | 60% | + €74 375 |
| Over €250 000 | | | 65% | + €2 500 |
| **3. Between uncles/aunts and nephews/nieces** | | | | |
| (the tax is calculated for the whole group at the following rates) | | | | |
| €0 | - | €50 000 | 35% | |
| €50 000 | - | €100 000 | 50% | + €17 500 |
| €100 000 | - | €175 000 | 60% | + €42 500 |
| Over €175 000 | | | 70% | + €87 500 |
| **4 Between other persons** | | | | |
| (the tax is calculated for the whole group at the following rates) | | | | |
| €0 | - | €50 000 | 40% | |
| €50 000 | - | €75 000 | 55% | + €20 000 |
| €75 000 | - | €175 000 | 65% | + €33 750 |
| over €175 000 | | | 80% | + €98 750 |

Legacies tot non-profit associations and foundations: 25% (12.5% if recognised as charitable institutions by the federal government).

# Flanders: Gift Tax

Gift tax on **movables** is calculated at the flat rate of 3% for donations between (grand)parents and (grand)children, spouses and registered partners and 7% for donations to anyone else.

Gift tax on **real property** is calculated on the value of the donation

| On the band between | | | Rate | Tax on previous bands |
|---|---|---|---|---|

**1 Direct line, spouses, registered partners**

| On the band between | | | Rate | Tax on previous bands |
|---|---|---|---|---|
| €0 | - | €12 500 | 3% | |
| €12 500 | - | €25 000 | 4% | + €375 |
| €25 000 | - | €50 000 | 5% | + €875 |
| €50 000 | - | €100 000 | 7% | + €2 125 |
| €100 000 | - | €150 000 | 10% | + €5 625 |
| €150 000 | - | €200 000 | 14% | + €10 625 |
| €200 000 | - | €250 000 | 18% | + €17 625 |
| €250 000 | - | €500 000 | 24% | + €26 625 |
| over €500 000 | | | 30% | + €86 625 |

**2 Between brothers and sisters**

| On the band between | | | Rate | Tax on previous bands |
|---|---|---|---|---|
| €0 | - | €12 500 | 20% | |
| €12 500 | - | €25 000 | 25% | + €2 500 |
| €25 000 | - | €75 000 | 35% | + €5 625 |
| €75 000 | - | €175 000 | 50% | + €23 125 |
| over €175 000 | | | 65% | + €73 125 |

**3. Between uncles/aunts and nephews/nieces**

| On the band between | | | Rate | Tax on previous bands |
|---|---|---|---|---|
| €0 | - | €12 500 | 25% | |
| €12 500 | - | €25 000 | 30% | + €3 125 |
| €25 000 | - | €75 000 | 40% | + €6 875 |
| €75 000 | - | €175 000 | 55% | + €26 875 |
| over €175 000 | | | 70% | + €81 875 |

**4 Between other persons**

| On the band between | | | Rate | Tax on previous bands |
|---|---|---|---|---|
| €0 | - | €12 500 | 30% | |
| €12 500 | - | €25 000 | 35% | + €3 750 |
| €25 000 | - | €75 000 | 50% | + €8 125 |
| €75 000 | - | €175 000 | 65% | + €33 125 |
| over €175 000 | | | 80% | + €98 125 |

Donations to non-profit associations and foundations (in Belgium or in the European Economic Area): 7%.

# Flanders: Inheritance Tax

Inheritance tax is calculated, for each heir separately, on his share of the estate

| On the band between | | Rate | Tax on previous bands |
|---|---|---|---|

**1 Direct line, spouses, registered partners, cohabitating partners**

| | | | |
|---|---|---|---|
| €0 - €50 000 | | 3% | |
| €50 000 - €250 000 | | 9% | + €1 500 |
| Over €250 000 | | 27% | + €19 500 |

The tax is calculated separately for real estate and moveable assets.

Liabilities are set off against moveable assets, unless they were specifically incurred to acquire real estate

**2 Between brothers and sisters**

| | | | |
|---|---|---|---|
| €0 - €75 000 | | 30% | |
| €75 000 - €125 000 | | 55% | + €22 500 |
| Over €125 000 | | 65% | + €50 000 |

**3. Between other persons**
**(the tax is calculated for the whole group at the following rates)**

| | | | |
|---|---|---|---|
| €0 - €75 000 | | 45% | |
| €75 000 - €125 000 | | 55% | + €33 750 |
| Over €125 000 | | 65% | + €61 250 |

Legacies tot non-profit associations and foundations (in Belgium or within the European Economic Area): 8.8%.

# Wallonia: Gift Tax

Gift tax on **movables** is calculated at the flat rate of 3.3% for donations between (grand)parents and (grand)children, spouses and registered partners, 5.5% between brothers and sisters and uncles or aunts and nephews or nieces and 7.7% for donations to anyone else.

Gift tax on **real property** is calculated on the value of the donation

| On the band between | | | Rate | Tax on previous bands |
|---|---|---|---|---|

**1 Direct line, spouses, registered partners**

| On the band between | | | Rate | Tax on previous bands |
|---|---|---|---|---|
| €0 | - | €12 500 | 3% | |
| €12 500 | - | €25 000 | 4% | + €375 |
| €25 000 | - | €50 000 | 5% | + €875 |
| €50 000 | - | €100 000 | 7% | + €2 125 |
| €100 000 | - | €150 000 | 10% | + €5 625 |
| €150 000 | - | €200 000 | 14% | + €10 625 |
| €200 000 | - | €250 000 | 18% | + €17 625 |
| €250 000 | - | €500 000 | 24% | + €26 625 |
| over €500 000 | | | 30% | + €86 625 |

**2 Between brothers and sisters**

| On the band between | | | Rate | Tax on previous bands |
|---|---|---|---|---|
| €0 | - | €12 500 | 20% | |
| €12 500 | - | €25 000 | 25% | + €2 500 |
| €25 000 | - | €75 000 | 35% | + €5 625 |
| €75 000 | - | €175 000 | 50% | + €23 125 |
| over €175 000 | | | 65% | + €73 125 |

**3. Between uncles/aunts and nephews/nieces**

| On the band between | | | Rate | Tax on previous bands |
|---|---|---|---|---|
| €0 | - | €12 500 | 25% | |
| €12 500 | - | €25 000 | 30% | + €3 125 |
| €25 000 | - | €75 000 | 40% | + €6 875 |
| €75 000 | - | €175 000 | 55% | + €26 875 |
| over €175 000 | | | 70% | + €81 875 |

**4 Between other persons**

| On the band between | | | Rate | Tax on previous bands |
|---|---|---|---|---|
| €0 | - | €12 500 | 30% | |
| €12 500 | - | €25 000 | 35% | + €3 750 |
| €25 000 | - | €75 000 | 60% | + €8 125 |
| €75 000 | - | €175 000 | 80% | + €38 125 |
| over €175 000 | | | 80% | + €118 125 |

Donations to non-profit associations and foundations (in Belgium or in the European Economic Area): 7%.

# Wallonia: Inheritance Tax

Inheritance tax is calculated, for each heir separately, on his share

| On the band between | | | Rate | Tax on previous bands |
|---|---|---|---|---|
| **1 Direct line, spouses, registered partners** | | | | |
| €0 | - | €12 500 | 3% | |
| €12 500 | - | €25 000 | 4% | +   €375 |
| €25 000 | - | €50 000 | 5% | +   €875 |
| €50 000 | - | €100 000 | 7% | + €2 125 |
| €100 000 | - | €150 000 | 10% | + €5 625 |
| €150 000 | - | €200 000 | 14% | + €10 625 |
| €200 000 | - | €250 000 | 18% | + €17 625 |
| €250 000 | - | €500 000 | 24% | + €26 625 |
| over €500 000 | | | 30% | + €86 625 |
| **2 Between brothers and sisters** | | | | |
| €0 | - | €12 500 | 20% | |
| €12 500 | - | €25 000 | 25% | + €2 500 |
| €25 000 | - | €75 000 | 35% | + €5 625 |
| €75 000 | - | €175 000 | 50% | + €23 125 |
| over €175 000 | | | 65% | + €73 125 |
| **3. Between uncles/aunts and nephews/nieces** | | | | |
| €0 | - | €12 500 | 25% | |
| €12 500 | - | €25 000 | 30% | + €3 125 |
| €25 000 | - | €75 000 | 40% | + €6 875 |
| €75 000 | - | €175 000 | 55% | + €26 875 |
| over €175 000 | | | 70% | + €81 875 |
| **4 Between other persons** | | | | |
| €0 | - | €12 500 | 30% | |
| €12 500 | - | €25 000 | 35% | + €3 750 |
| €25 000 | - | €75 000 | 60% | + €8 125 |
| over €175 000 | | | 80% | + €38 125 |

Legacies to non-profit associations and foundations (in Belgium or in the European Economic Area: 7%.